THE AUTHOR

John de Gruchy is Professor of Christian Studies at the University of Cape Town. He is a minister in the United Congregational Church of Southern Africa. From 1968-1973 he was Director of Studies and Communication at the Southern African Council of Churches. He is editor of the *Journal of Theology for Southern Africa*.

Professor de Gruchy's teaching and research is mainly concerned with Christian Studies and the Church in Southern Africa, and reflects his long-standing concern with Dietrich Bonhoeffer. His recent publication *Bonhoeffer and South Africa: Theology in Dialogue* (London and Grand Rapids, 1984) is one of the many fruits of this study. He is executive member of the International Bonhoeffer Society for Archive and Research. Other publications include *The Church Struggle in South Africa* (Grand Rapids, Cape Town and London, 1979) and *Apartheid is a Heresy* (Cape Town, Grand Rapids, 1982), of which he is coeditor.

CRY JUSTICE!

Prayers, meditations and readings from South Africa

JOHN W. DE GRUCHY

Foreword by Bishop Desmond Tutu

Illustrations by Patrick Holo

ORBIS BOOKS

Maryknoll, New York 10545

First published in Great Britain by Collins Liturgical Publications, 8 Grafton Street, London W1X 3LA, and in the United States by Orbis Books Maryknoll, NY 10545

Copyright © 1986 by John de Gruchy

Manufactured in Great Britain

ORBIS/ISBN 0-88344-223-X

CONTENTS

Contents

ILLUSTRATIONS

NOTE ON THE ARTIST

PATRICK HOLO lives and works in Nyanga, a black township near Crossroads on the outskirts of metropolitan Cape Town. He was born in Nyanga in 1948, the eldest in a family of six. On the death of his father, Patrick was unable to continue his education as he became responsible for the welfare of his family. In 1971, after much hardship and struggle, he finally began to fulfil an early yearning to work as an artist. That same year, together with some fellow artists, he established the Nyanga Art Centre which has since gained a widespread reputation for its contribution to African art. It was not until 1981, however, that Patrick had any formal education in graphics, at the University of Cape Town, and then in 1982, having won a scholarship from the Italian government, he studied at the University of Bella Arte Academico in Perugia. On his return to South Africa he continued to work and teach at the Nyanga Art Centre, and it was there that he produced the illustrations for this volume.

The illustrations are the result of Patrick Holo's reflections on the content of this book in relation to everyday life in a black township as he experiences and perceives it. Patrick has the ability to blend religious symbols and daily life in a natural yet profound and often powerful way. Indeed, the striking realism of his work often reflects the pain and frustration of his community as well as its humanity, its caring, and its hope, in the light of the Incarnation, Cross and Resurrection.

Patrick Holo's work has been exhibited in several exhibitions both in South Africa and overseas. This is the first occasion, however, in which he has illustrated a book. It is his wish to dedicate these graphics to his mother 'without whom I would not have achieved my sincere ambitions'.

To all, both far and near
who hope and pray, struggle and suffer
in order to celebrate justice and peace
in South Africa

FOREWORD

Christians, being eucharistic people, will want to give thanks for much that we owe to the ancients, especially the Greeks with their art and literature as well as their philosophy. But in one respect they have left us a legacy which has turned out to be a baneful influence on western thought and attitudes. I refer here to the hellenistic dualism which caused them to have a penchant for separating this from that and splitting things up into the material and the spiritual that turned out to be ensconced in watertight compartments. The spiritual tended to be that category of things which were considered good intrinsically, while those material were regarded as by their very nature evil. The twain would never meet.

Western Christendom has had an extra dose of this metaphysical dualism through Augustine of Hippo who, during his spiritual pilgrimage from paganism to his conversion to Christianity, had occasion to dabble with Manichaeism.

It is from these sources that Westerners have derived their extraordinary capacity to conceive of improper dichotomies as between the so-called sacred and the secular, the profane and the holy, the material and the spiritual. It is ultimately from this hellenistic foundation that we have obtained what has come to be a favourite parrot cry 'Don't mix religion with politics'.

Some time ago Archbishop Runcie, the Archbishop of Canterbury, incensed many in the English Establishment for preaching a sermon in St Paul's Cathedral at a service to celebrate the British victory over Argentine. He upset people because he did not preach a sufficiently jingoistic sermon. In fact he spoke far too favourably of the Argentinians. The Church of England was never more talked about than when during the miners' crippling strike, some of the English bishops had the audacity to suggest that Mrs. Thatcher's monetarist policies might be immoral and the cause of so much unemployment. It was then that the Church of England was accused of interfering in an area for which she had not competence. One Government MP actually used an occasion when he was preaching in a University Church to read the Church the riot act about mixing politics with religion.

It never ceases to amaze me that the Church or its leaders are almost invariably accused of this heinous crime when they condemn a particular sociopolitical or economic dispensation (or some feature of it) as being unjust or oppressive. If we were to stand up and say we did not think apartheid was too bad really, then you can bet your bottom dollar that hardly any of our erstwhile critics would accuse us of meddling in politics.

Africans, consistent with the biblical tradition, do not accept improper dichotomies. For them life is of a piece and the spiritual and the material inform each other quite intimately. It is a deeply spiritual matter the question of the relationship between a husband and wife. In South Africa it becomes a political and moral issue when it is a crime for a man to sleep with his wife because he is a migrant worker who is prevented from bringing his wife and children where he works; ironically black family life is undermined by state policy in a country that actually has a public holiday dedicated to the sanctity of the family.

When religion sanctifies the unjust status quo it is not being meddlesome politically. Helder Camara said 'When I ask for bread for the poor then they praise me. When I ask why the poor are hungry then they say I am a communist.'

Africans are on the whole religious and so you will have our political meetings and rallies opened with prayer and closed with the singing of our national anthems (contained in this book), which are not chauvinistic compositions calling for our triumph over our enemies who should be confounded, but are supplications asking God to bless Africa and her children.

For many of us it is not our politics that constrains us to say and do what we do and say in opposition to apartheid and in working for a new South Africa. It is precisely our relationship with God, it is our worship, our meditation, our attendance at the Eucharist, it is these spiritual things which compel us to speak up for God, 'Thus saith the Lord . . .', to be the voice of the voiceless. For many of us the spiritual is utterly central to all we are and do and say. It is precisely because we are turned first to God that he constrains us to turn towards our neighbour.

And so I am thankful to John de Gruchy for this anthology which seeks to help all who want such help (and who does not?) so that we can be God's fellow workers, his agents to transfigure South Africa.

In this struggle for justice, peace and reconciliation the Christian resources are ultimately spiritual. We are thankful that Prof. de Gruchy has illustrated this to be the case. We are not motivated by a few agitators.

Desmond Tutu
Bishop of Johannesburg
November 1985

Meditations, Reflections and Prayers

For Use Alone or in Community

Over the years of my stumbling pilgrimage in Christian faith and life I have been greatly helped, challenged and enriched by what were once called 'manuals of devotion'. Some of these have been very traditional, classics of the spiritual life, others have been more contemporary in style and theme. But without doubt they have often come to my rescue in moments of dryness and doubt. One of the classics is the seventeenth century *A Guide to Prayer* by Isaac Watts, father of English hymnody and writer of the hymn, 'When I survey the wondrous cross'. Towards the end of his *Guide*, Watts provides some rules on 'the matter of prayer', one of which is this:

> If we find our hearts, after all, very barren, and hardly know how to frame a prayer before God of ourselves, it has been oftentimes useful to take a book in our hand, wherein are contained some spiritual meditations in a petitionary form, some devout reflections, or excellent patterns of prayer; and above all, the Psalms of David, some of the Prophecies of Isaiah, some chapters in the Gospels, or any of the Epistles.[1]

While I would hesitate to suggest that this book of medita-

---

[1] Isaac Watts *A Guide to Prayer*, edited by Harry Escott, Epworth, London. 1948, p.53.

tions, reflections and prayers, ranks in any way with the volumes to which I have referred, it does belong to the same genre. Yet it is different in certain important respects. Consideration of the similarities and differences will introduce my intention in compiling it, and also provide some suggestions for its use.

Firstly, it is quite deliberately set within the context of South Africa. There have been other devotional books written by South Africans, not least those by the Dutch Reformed church leader and holiness preacher Andrew Murray. But to the best of my knowledge, with the exception of Alan Paton's *Instrument of Thy Peace*[2], these could have been written in any location: they do not arise out of the South African situation as such[3]. What I have attempted is to provide material that is specifically rooted in this context. My intention is that devotional reflection should arise out of and focus upon the South African situation. Hopefully this will provide some new perspectives for South Africans who use it, and enable those beyond our borders to share our struggles, fears and hopes as they worship, pray and act.

Inasmuch as South Africa is not unique but a microcosm of the world, the readings and prayers in the book have universal significance. The struggle for justice, liberation and peace, against racism, oppression and violence, are worldwide. It is therefore my hope that the book will serve a wider purpose than simply focusing prayerful attention on South Africa. Indeed, it is my conviction that reflection on situations other than our own enables us to discern factors within our context which would otherwise remain hidden.

Not all the material has been written by South Africans, but virtually all has been written from within the South African context, and generally by people who have identified themselves fully with its life. The material is taken from a wide variety of sources, old and new, and representing

[2] Alan Paton, *Instrument of Thy Peace*, Seabury, New York, 1968.
[3] David Bosch's *A Spirituality for the Road,* Herald Press, Scottdale, 1979, while a South African contribution to the spirituality of mission, is not specifically rooted in the South African situation.

many different Christian traditions. Catholics and Protestants, Charismatics and Pentecostalists, black and white, women and men, are all represented. Yet I have not included them in order to be representative, but because what they have said is of importance for us today. Although my own roots are Free Church and Reformed, being a minister of the United Congregational Church, I have been enriched by the spirituality of many different traditions, including Eastern Orthodoxy which, while largely absent from South Africa, in some striking ways resembles African Christianity. While each tradition has its own distinct character, at their best they all converge in enabling true worship and discipleship.

Secondly, most if not all of the classic manuals of devotion, and much of their more contemporary heirs, are primarily for the use of individuals in solitude and alone. This volume is intended for private use, and I will make some suggestions in that regard in a moment. But I have designed it in such a way that it can also be used within Christian community. The final set of readings is, in fact, an Agape or 'love feast' which is clearly intended to be celebrated with others when, for some reason, it is not possible to share in an eucharistic celebration.

For some years now my wife and I have participated week by week in one of the 'house churches' which belong to the congregation of which we are members. I have had this small community of Christians in mind as I have prepared this book. From comments I have received, I feel confident that it could be of help and value as a resource for community reflection, discussion, prayer and worship. I believe it could be a helpful resource for use on retreats, and may even provide additional readings and prayers within the context of the Sunday liturgy.

Thirdly, books of this kind, and mine is no exception, invariably include passages of scripture and prayers; many also contain readings either written by the author or culled from other sources. Often these readings are verses of hymns or what St Paul called 'spiritual songs'. But they are usually intended for reflection or for 'making melody in the heart', not for singing out aloud. From an African perspective, however, it is almost inconceivable to pray without at some point bursting into song. I have therefore included hymns and songs to be used as they were intended, as corporate acts of praise or petition. For this reason the music also has been incorporated in the text.

All of the hymns and songs are South African, though they are invariably based on passages of scripture in the best tradition of Christian hymnody. With a few exceptions, they all originate within the black Christian community and have already proved themselves in the context of worship. I would encourage those who are unfamiliar with African music and hymnody to persevere in learning what are simple, beautiful and often haunting melodies and perhaps even learn to sing them in the original language, though an English translation is always given. In some measure this may contribute to the cross-cultural exposure which all of us need in the modern world, especially if we claim to belong to the universal church of Jesus Christ.

Fourthly, as already mentioned, all the sections include substantial readings from scripture. Christian prayer and worship is rooted in the Bible and arises out of hearing and reflecting on the Word of God as it is read and proclaimed. Christian devotion can go off into all kinds of dubious and unhealthy directions when sundered from the biblical tradition. Of central importance in this regard, as Isaac Watts notes, are the psalms, for they embody human response to divine revelation in a wide range of communal, personal and historical situations.

Amongst the other readings in this book there is, however, material that is not explicitly Christian, some which is critical of the church, and some which is secular and political. My purpose in selecting and including such material is to ensure that our Christian devotion remains related to reality and does not become a way of escape into some ghetto of pseudo-piety. It is often the non-Christian critic, whether poet, dramatist, painter or author, who most powerfully perceives reality, refusing to allow us to run away and hide, confronting us with raw experiences of pain, doubt and anger, and calling us back to reality and to our responsibility as Christians in the world. Prayer is as much dependent upon reading the newspaper and participating in the struggles and agonies of life as it is upon its traditional resources.

Fifthly, this volume differs from most other manuals of devotion because, as I have already intimated, it is quite explicitly focused on the South African situation. Several things should be noted in this regard. In South Africa, where the overwhelming number of the population claim some allegiance to a Christian church, eighty-eight percent of all church members are black.[4] It might be said, then, that the church in South Africa is a black church with some white members. Of course, the church situation is more complex than this bald statement suggests, but it would be quite unrelated to reality if a book such as this did not reflect the African character of the Christian tradition in South Africa. This I have attempted to do at the very outset, and by the use of African artwork as well as the hymns already mentioned.

Christianity must never be allowed to become captive to culture, but it cannot exist except in meaningful relation to it. Furthermore, Christian faith and spirituality cannot be sundered from the struggles, hopes and fears of people and nations. In South Africa this means, above all else, that a book such as this has to be grounded to a large degree in the struggle against the heresy of apartheid, and in the struggle for justice, liberation, reconciliation and peace. Some themes that might well find their place in a book of devotional readings in other circumstances are therefore absent. As there is no lack of such material available, there is no need for this volume to attempt to cover everything related to Christian spirituality, or for that matter to the South African situation.

In an introductory essay I discuss more fully how I understand the relationship between prayer and politics, spirituality and social transformation. I regard it as of the greatest importance that this relationship be affirmed and properly

---

[4] See my essay 'Christians in Conflict: the Social Reality of the South African Church', *Journal of Theology for Southern Africa*, no. 51, June 1985.

understood. Moreover, despite the variety and nature of the material I have selected for the readings, the essay also seeks to show that there is an underlying, theological coherence to what I have attempted, derived from the biblical proclamation of the kingdom of God revealed in Jesus Christ. While this provides a theological framework for the readings as I understand them, it is not intended as a straightjacket for the user.

Finally, then, how can the book be used as a manual of private devotion? There are thirty-one sets of readings, sufficient that is for a month's use, on a variety of themes. These are followed by an Agape or 'love-feast' which is obviously a corporate act of worship. The overall structure of the readings should be obvious from the table of contents, and this will become clearer to the user. It may help to mention at the outset that they generally follow the traditional pattern of Christian belief, starting with God as creator and redeemer of the world and its peoples, then exploring aspects of the journey of Christian faith, life and community, and finally reaching toward the future coming of God's reign.

Each set of readings focuses upon a particular theme, which is introduced by a statement about the Christian life in relation to it. Scripture readings which ground the theme in the biblical tradition then follow. Poetry, theological meditations, and other readings explore the theme further, often concluding with a hymn or an acclamation of praise. Some of the readings, or sets of readings, may well be too long for the amount of time available. If this is so, then it simply means that a set of readings may be used over several days, bound together by a common theme. Hopefully the readings, the hymns and the artwork will stir the imagination into fresh and more personally meaningful directions which will aid prayer and praise and result in greater commitment to Jesus Christ as Lord in the service of the good news of the kingdom of God in the world today.

Apartheid is abhorrent to any person who has proper regard for moral values let alone those who take Christian ethics seriously. It is beyond reform. Peace and reconciliation in South Africa will only come about through the development of just social structures in which every person freely participates as a human being. Since this manuscript was originally submitted for publication a great deal has happened in South Africa to demonstrate the dehumanizing and destructive character of apartheid. Protest has been violently repressed and, in turn, has evoked angry and often violent response. Amidst intense suffering, anger and bitterness, the cry for justice has become even stronger and more determined. It is difficult to capture all this, especially its immediacy and agony, in print. In the nature of the case, it is impossible to produce a book which is up to date, and the rapid acceleration of events in South Africa make this even more difficult than is normally the case. May I suggest, therefore, that while using this book you also gather your own resources relating to both the South African and to your own situation so that your reflection, prayer and action remains relevant.

It is difficult to name everyone who has helped me in preparing this book, but I am grateful to all. I would, however, especially mention Stephanie Shutte and David Russell, my colleagues Charles Villa-Vicencio, Gabriel Setiloane and Bill Domeris, and Kevin Garcia, a graduate assistant, in the Department of Religious Studies, my brother-in-law Ron Steel, and my elder son Stephen (Steve to his friends). Their comments and suggestions have helped to make the book much better than it would have been. A special word of thanks must go to Fr. Dave Dargie of the Lumko Pastoral Institute for his enthusiastic and expert help with the African hymns, and to Patrick Holo for his illustrations. As always, Nan Oosthuizen shared her secretarial skills warmly and willingly, and also compiled the index. The idea of the book has been inside me for several years. But the catalyst who spurred me to action earlier this year was Tom Longford of William Collins (London). What I proposed was enthusiastically supported by Sue Chapman at Collins who has continued to encourage and enable the completion of the project.

It is easy to take the support of my wife, Isobel, for granted because it is always present. But I deeply appreciate it, as well as that of the rest of my family.

John W. de Gruchy
Cape Town
September 1985

Christian Spirituality and Social Transformation

A South African Perspective

Piety, spirituality, and the Christian life

Piety is widely suspect because it has come to mean a way of escape from responsible living in the real world. True piety is something else. It is life lived in devotion to God and service of others. Christian piety at its best has made a significant contribution to the social transformation of the world. The tragedy is that piety can so easily turn in on itself and degenerate into an unhealthy and neurotic legalism which denies the transformative power of the gospel in the life of individuals and society.[5] In becoming deaf to the cry for justice and blind to the plight of the poor, such pseudo-piety sanctions injustice and applies brakes to just social change. It is therefore contrary to the proclamation of the good news that God's kingdom has come in Jesus Christ.

The concept 'spirituality', which in large measure has replaced that of 'piety', has wider contemporary acceptance, though it is also not without its critics.[6] For many Christians it sounds esoteric, an artificial technique to acquire sanctity, something to do with transcendental meditation, yoga or even spiritualism. For some Protestants it immediately suggests a return to a form of monastic devotion and asceticism, medieval mysticism, the climbing of a heavenly ladder

---

[5] See W. Pannenberg, *Christian Spirituality*, Westminster, Philadelphia, 1983, pp.13ff.
[6] See E.J. Tinsley, *The Imitation of God in Christ: an Essay in the Biblical Basis of Christian Spirituality*, SCM, London, 1960, p.13ff.

through a combination of penitential prayer and good works. This kind of spirituality can obstruct that knowledge of God which comes through faith in Jesus Christ and is evidenced in the costly discipleship of love and hope.

Precisely because the word 'spirituality' is so ambiguous and confusing, theologians ranging from the Russian Orthodox Alexander Schmemann to the Swiss Reformed Karl Barth have preferred to speak more simply and directly about 'the Christian life'. That is, the whole of life 'renewed, transformed and transfigured by the Holy Spirit'.[7] In agreement with them I have prefaced every set of readings in this book with a short statement on the Christian life.

The term 'spirituality' nevertheless remains useful. At one level it refers to the character or ethos of the Christian tradition as it has taken root and flourished within particular Christian communities in different cultural and historical contexts. This is of special interest to us because our focus is on spirituality within the South African context. At another level, spirituality is about those disciplines which enable the flourishing of Christian life, community and witness.

Many helpful disciplines have emerged in the history of Christian spirituality to aid growth in the Spirit. Sometimes these disciplines have been abused, resulting in the crippling of Christian life. They have also been misunderstood as a means to guarantee the achievement of holiness, or as intended for spiritual elites only. When properly understood and used they remain of considerable value for all who are committed to the Christian life-style, and some, like the discipline of prayer, are indispensable.[8] True Christian spirituality, and therefore the proper use of the disciplines of the spiritual life, refers to the enabling of all Christians, not just those with a particular religious vocation, to trust and follow Jesus Christ more faithfully.

The Christian life begins with God's gracious acceptance

---

[7] Schmemann quoted by Gordon Wakefield, *Westminster Dictionary of Christian Spirituality*, p.362. See Karl Barth, *The Christian Life: Church Dogmatics IV14*, T&T Clark, Edinburgh, 1981, p.92f. et.al.

[8] For useful contemporary exposition of these disciplines, see Richard Foster, *The Celebration of Discipline*, Hodder and Stoughton, London, 1980.

of us in Jesus Christ. This acceptance becomes personal through our response of obedient faith and our baptism into the community of faith, the church. It is expressed in a life of deepening trust and obedient discipleship in the midst of the world. Its direction is the transformation of the whole of life so that we are increasingly set free by the Spirit to reflect the glory of Jesus Christ as Lord over all creation and all of life (cf. 2 Corinthians 3:17f). Christian spirituality concerns the means of grace whereby this process of transformation becomes a reality in our lives and society.

The Christian life, while intensely personal, is always communal. Christian life is formed and shaped by participation in the life of the church. At the heart of Christian spirituality is an ecclesial experience, that common life of prayer, listening to the Word of God, eucharistic worship, fellowship and witness in the world which characterised the first Christian community (cf. Acts 2:42f). In some circumstances, prison for example, Christians might be forced to live alone, or they might even choose to be alone in prayer for the sake of others. But the privatization of piety is not part of the Christian tradition and it undermines the Christian life. Indeed, when Christians are forced by circumstances to live separated from Christian community they discover how much a part of the 'body of Christ' they really are.

This common life which Christians share together is a reality greater than the sum of its individual members; it is a gift of grace, life shared in Christ with all who believe. Christian spirituality is, therefore, the spirituality of Christian community. But it is not Christian community lived in isolation from the world, the spirituality of the pious ghetto. Neither is it separate from the life of the church as a whole. Amongst his many perceptive insights on the nature of Christian community is Dietrich Bonhoeffer's reminder that

life together under the Word will remain sound and healthy only where it does not form itself into a movement, an order, a society, a *collegium pietatis*, but rather where it understands itself as being a part of the one, holy, catholic, Christian Church, where it shares actively and passively in the sufferings and struggles and promise of the whole church.[9]

This means, amongst other things, that Christian spirituality has to do with the constant renewal of the church itself in the power of the Spirit. It also means that its focus is not primarily the perfection of the soul but the mission of the church in the world. Christian spirituality enables the Christian alone and in community to witness to the kingdom of God in Jesus Christ.

Spirituality of the kingdom

A reading of the gospels can leave us in no doubt that the kingdom of God is the central theme of Jesus' ministry, and that his call to discipleship is an invitation to live life under the reign of God.[10] The Christian life is above all else one of discipleship enabled by the grace of the Spirit and lived in response to the reign of God which has been established in the world in the coming of Jesus the Messiah. Jesus beckons us to follow him in the midst of the world in obedient action and prayerful expectation of the promised 'new heaven and new earth'. 'Biblical spirituality' writes Albert Nolan, 'is kingdom spirituality. To be moved and motivated by the Spirit of Jesus is to be moved and motivated by an all-absorbing concern for the coming of God's kingdom.'[11] At the heart of kingdom spirituality is the prayer of Jesus: 'Your kingdom come, your will be done on earth, as it is in heaven' (Matthew 6:10).

It is a truncated and therefore false understanding of the kingdom of God when it is regarded as referring solely to life after death in heaven. When Jesus speaks about the kingdom of God, or, as in the gospel according to Matthew, the kingdom of heaven, he is referring to God's universal reign

---

[9] D. Bonhoeffer, *Life Together*, Harper & Row, New York, 1954, p.37.

[10] See, inter alia, Joachim Jeremias, *New Testament Theology*, Vol. 1, SCM, London, 1971.

[11] Albert Nolan OP, *Biblical Spirituality*, Order of Preachers, Springs, 1982, p.57.

over all reality, on earth and beyond.[12] Similarly, when Jesus tells Pilate that his 'kingdom is not of this world' (John 18:36) he is not saying that it has nothing to do with the world but that, unlike Pilate's rule, Jesus' authority is derived from God alone. The false spiritualising of the message of the kingdom is destructive of the biblical message and lies at the heart of pseudo-piety.

If the Christian life is understood from the perspective of the kingdom of God, then it embraces the whole of life and reality. Life can no longer be conceived as split into the sacred and profane, as though part of life belonged to God and the rest to some other realm or power. The separation of piety from life in the world no longer becomes tenable. For the Christian, all life is under the reign of God in Christ, whether this is acknowledged or not. This is the biblical vision, often forgotten in thought and practice with disastrous consequences, but always regained and affirmed in times of renewal and reformation. The Christian, wrote Dietrich Bonhoeffer,

> must therefore really live in the godless world, without attempting to gloss over or explain its ungodliness in some religious way or other. He must live a 'secular' life, and thereby share in God's sufferings. He *may* live a 'secular' life (as one who has been freed from false religious obligations and inhibitions). To be a Christian does not mean to be religious in a particular way, to make something of oneself (a sinner, a penitent, or a saint) on the basis of some method or other, but to be a man[13] — not a type of man , but the man that Christ creates in us. It is not the religious act that makes the Christian, but participation in the sufferings of God in the secular life. That is *metanoia*: not in the first place thinking about one's own needs, problems, sins, and fears, but allowing oneself to

---

[12] See B. Klappert, 'King, Kingdom' in Colin Brown (ed.) *The New International Dictionary of New Testament Theology*, Vol. 2, Paternoster, London, 1976, p.381f. Klappert's whole article is germane to this discussion.

[13] It should be noted that while I prefer to use inclusive language in my own writing, I have not taken the liberty of changing terms in the writings of others.

be caught up in the way of Jesus Christ, into the messianic event, thus fulfilling Isa. 53.[14]

The Christian life, and therefore Christian spirituality, is essentially a matter of *metanoia* not method. Nowhere is this transformation expressed more clearly than in Paul's Letter to the Romans:

> I urge you, brothers, in view of God's mercy, to offer your bodies as living sacrifices, holy and pleasing to God — which is your spiritual worship. Do not conform any longer to the pattern of this world, but be transformed by the renewing of your mind. Then you will be able to test and approve what God's will is — his good, pleasing and perfect will (12:1-2 NIV).

It is precisely this radical reorientation of life that Jesus has in mind when, conversing with Nicodemus the pharisee, he tells him of the need to be 'born again' if he is to 'see the kingdom of God' (John 3:3f.). Without such a fundamental change it is impossible to discern God's reign over all reality in Jesus the Messiah and so become part of the new age which has dawned in him.

Conversion, or our spiritual rebirth, means the reorientation of our lives so that we no longer live in conformity to the values and powers of the world, but become part of God's transforming purpose. Christian spirituality, as distinct from pseudo-piety, is about this transformation, a transformation which directly affects, even confronts, the life of the world in which we live. 'When we allow the Spirit of God to work in us we become critical of the world we live in, past and present, and we begin to strive for, hope for and long for God's future world of justice, love and freedom.'[15]

An inevitable concomitant of such a conversion is conflict and suffering. The reign of God in Jesus Christ brings both the Christian disciple and the Christian community, when faithful to the gospel, into confrontation with all that is con-

---

[14] Dietrich Bonhoeffer, *Letters and Papers from Prison*, Macmillan, New York, 1975, p.361f.
[15] Nolan, *op. cit.*

trary to it in society. The Christian life is depicted in the New Testament as a struggle against the 'principalities and powers of evil', against that force which shapes the values and norms of sinful humanity (see Ephesians 6:10ff.). A spirituality of the kingdom requires an acute sense of the all-pervasiveness of sin, that is, human pride and the will to power in opposition to the will of God. Sin is as much a social reality as it is personal, and the church has to take the reality of social evil with utter seriousness in its struggle to be faithful to Jesus Christ.[16]

Some readers of this essay and what follows might feel that certain key elements in Christian spirituality are absent or muted. I refer especially to such dimensions of the Christian life as joy, peace, and celebration. These are undoubtedly central to a spirituality of the kingdom and need to be affirmed. At the same time, like the equally important concepts of love, forgiveness and reconciliation, they have been debased through misuse and misunderstanding. When separated from a spirituality which is committed to justice they are cheapened and emptied of significance; they become symptoms of 'cheap grace' rather than the result of costly discipleship. In the midst of the struggle for justice, in truly seeking to follow Jesus Christ in the midst of the world, Christians will know a joy and deep peace which has its source in the Spirit. In the midst of pain, agony and despair, Christians committed to the coming kingdom can and do celebrate their hope and anticipate the victory of God's shalom. But the joy and feasting of Christian spirituality is always in the shadow of the cross and human suffering, and it cannot be separated from the struggle for justice and liberation.

The history of Christianity demonstrates that a faithful church suffers for its testimony to Jesus Christ. Jesus warned his disciples not to be surprised if the world hated them (John 15:18f.). This is because the gospel challenges the values which the world regards so highly: power, wealth,

---

[16] See Stephen Charles Mott, *Biblical Ethics and Social Change*, Oxford, New York, 1982, pp.3ff.

false pride whether personal or national, and the violence which is required to maintain them. The conflict between the church and the world is not, however, between the righteous and the unrighteous, as if the Christian community can claim to be anything other than unrighteous and sinful. The conflict is between the gospel of the kingdom of God, to which the church in its frailty and sin bears witness, and the world of which the church is a part. That is why the church can only bear prophetic witness to the world and the state when it is also repentant and humble, listening itself to the prophetic Word. A proud, triumphalistic church is a denial of the gospel because the kingdom of God is about the suffering servant, Jesus Christ.

The goal of the kingdom is not to make the church politically powerful but to redeem the world and make it more just. Precisely for this reason, a church which has ceased to proclaim the demands of God's kingdom amidst the concrete circumstances of its life in the world has sold out to the kingdoms of this world, betrayed its trust, and failed in its responsibility. It is in being faithful to the gospel of the kingdom, despite the conflict, that the church serves the world as light and salt. It is only when the church conforms to the world that it becomes acceptable and comfortable within it, but then it no longer represents and bears witness to the kingdom of God. Its spirituality has become false; it has lost its saltiness (Matthew 5:13).

From the perspective of the kingdom of God personal and social transformation belong together and it is totally false and unbiblical to suggest that they can be separated. God's will and purpose is not only the transformation of our own lives and relationships but also the transformation and renewal of society. True spirituality, then, enables Christians to bear a more faithful witness to the whole gospel of the reign of God in Jesus Christ. It refuses to be side-tracked into those sterile discussions which debate whether the horizontal or the vertical, the personal or the social, has priority. The only priority for the Christian is 'to seek first God's kingdom and his righteousness' (Matthew 6:33) in every realm of life. The Archbishop of Durban, Denis Hurley, described the direction of Roman Catholic spirituality set by Vatican II when he wrote:

> From a Catholic spirituality dominated in the past by the monastic ideal of renunciation of the world for the sake of the kingdom, we have come a long way to seeing this world as an essential part of what must be transformed into this kingdom.[17]

In similar vein, but from a Protestant perspective, Wolfhart Pannenberg writes:

> traditional penitential pietism, its lasting influence in Protestant theology and spirituality notwithstanding, is unfit as a truly contemporary form of Christian piety that could claim to embody the spirit of liberation that has motivated and accompanied the gospel proclamation throughout history.[18]

Bearing witness to the reign of God in the world does not mean that we are able to 'bring in the kingdom of God'; that remains God's prerogative. But it does mean that we may become agents of change in the hands of God, and that is what the spirituality of the kingdom is about.

> The awareness that we cannot build a perfect society in history must not deflect us from the obligation to work for a better society. We would not think of postponing personal righteousness — sexual purity, for example — on the grounds that perfection will not come until after the Second Coming.[19]

Through prayer and listening to the Word of God, alone or in community, Christians begin to see reality from the perspective of the kingdom and so place themselves at the disposal of the God whose purposes are worked out in history. 'Christian meditation and contemplation' writes Jurgen Moltmann, 'lead us to discover our own self as a self

[17] Denis E. Hurley, 'Beyers Naude — Calvanist and Catholic', in Peter Randall (ed.) *Not without Honour: Tribute to Beyers Naude*, Ravan, Johannesburg, 1982, p.79.

[18] Pannenberg, *op. cit.*, p.29.

[19] Stephen Charles Mott, *Biblical Ethics and Social Change, op. cit.*, p.19.

accepted, freed, and redeemed by God in the comprehensive context of his history with the world. When we meditate upon Christ's history and through the Spirit experience our own history with Christ, we find not only ourselves, but also our place and our personal tasks within God's history with the world.'[20]

Prayer, social action and liberation

During the sixties there was a tendency amongst Christian social activists to relegate prayer and worship to the bottom of their agenda. Spirituality was regarded as a form of escapism, not a way of involvement. But activism alone produced spiritual emptiness, resulting either in a loss of faith or the discovery of spiritual renewal and experience in movements such as the charismatic, or even outside of the Christian tradition. In Jesus' teaching on the kingdom, prayer is quite central, simply because anyone who is seeking to witness faithfully to the gospel soon becomes aware of his or her dependence upon God. Prayer is, amongst other things, an expression of that relationship.

Most Christians have yet to discover the relationship between prayer and social action. As Richard Lovelace aptly comments: 'most of those who pray are not praying about social issues, and most of those who are active in social issues are not praying very much.'[21] This false dichotomy reflects a flawed understanding of both prayer and Christian social action stemming in the first instance from some of the basic misunderstandings of the gospel of the kingdom of God to which I have already referred. It is noteworthy that an increasing number of contemporary conservative evangelicals, like Lovelace, have shown the integral relationship between evangelical piety, evangelism and social action. [22] Stephen Mott puts it succinctly:

[20] Jurgen Moltmann, *The Open Church: Invitation to a Messianic Life-Style*, SCM, London, 1978, p.45f.

[21] Richard Lovelace, *Dynamics of Spiritual Life: An Evangelical Theology of Renewal*, IVP, Downers Grove, 1979, p.392.

[22] See John Stott, *Issues Facing Christians Today*, Marshalls, London, 1984, pp.2ff.; Jim Wallis, *A Call to Conversion*, Harper and Row, New York, 1982; a South African perspective is Michael Cassidy, *Bursting the Wineskins*, Hodder & Stoughton, London, 1983, see especially pp.192ff.

Vigorous and systematic social involvement requires not that Christians weaken the structure of their piety but rather that they carry it through to its natural social consequences.[23]

In South Africa the struggle against apartheid and injustice has often had a religious and Christian dimension. Particularly in recent years some of the traditional disciplines of spirituality, such as prayer and fasting, have become an integral part of that struggle. Prayer vigils and political protest have brought spirituality and social action together in opposition to apartheid. Perhaps the most public and radical expression of this connection between religious conviction and political struggle has been demonstrated at the funeral services of people who have died as a result of the struggle for liberation. But the full story has yet to be told of the courage, commitment, and spiritual depth of the many South Africans, black and white, young and old, who have suffered greatly, not least in prison and in solitary confinement, for their faith and conscience.

Yet it is also true that the Christian sanctification of apartheid, and the unbiblical privatization of piety which has separated prayer and the struggle for justice, has led many to reject Christianity as irrelevant at best and, at worst, as an obstacle to liberation. This rejection is expressed in several of the poems in this volume, but it is more powerfully demonstrated by the fact that for many people, especially younger blacks, the teaching of Karl Marx holds out more promise for the future than the message proclaimed and acted out by the churches. Instead of reacting in horror, Christians and especially white Christians should recognise their responsibility for this rejection of the gospel. It has largely been our apathy and indifference towards human rights and dignity, justice and freedom, which has brought it about. This volume is intended as a small contribution to the challenging of such indifference, and as a resource manual for transforming piety into a discipleship which is committed to the struggle for a just South Africa.

[23] Stephen Charles Mott, *op. cit.*, p.20.

In the service of the kingdom of God prayer and action in the world belong together. This is not something new, but rooted in biblical tradition and the history of Christianity. Even those medieval mystics who are so often regarded as having withdrawn from social responsibility knew that contemplation and action cannot be separated.[24] The unknown fourteenth century author of *The Cloud of Unknowing*, who so strongly advocated the contemplative life, remarked that a person 'cannot be fully active except he be partly contemplative, nor fully contemplative (at least on earth) without being partly active'.[25]

At the beginning of the seventies Segundo Galilea noted, in his own Latin American context, a reversal of the trend whereby activists shunned spirituality:

> I believe that there really is a spiritual awakening, precisely among those Christians who have committed themselves to the cause of liberation. Of late, there have been solid and widespread indications that many of them are rediscovering the meaning of faith and of prayer and doing so through their very commitment. The 'contemplative' is beginning to rediscover his place among the 'militants'.[26]

Prayer became necessary in the midst of social action in order to give it direction and meaning.[27]

Thomas Merton, who perhaps more than any other has attempted to relate prayer, contemplation and social action, perceptively argues that action sundered from contemplation ends up in ego-centred ambition and aggression, the confusion of ends and means, and the misuse of power. While the following comment refers specifically to the renewal of the church, within the context of Merton's own

---

[24] See Ray C. Petry, 'Social Responsibility and the Late Medieval Mystics', *Church History*, volume 21, March 1952, pp.3-19.

[25] *The Cloud of Unknowing*, Penguin, London, 1961, p.63.

[26] Segundo Galilea, 'Spiritual Awakening and Movements of Liberation in Latin America', *Concilium 9/9/*, November 1973, p.131.

[27] Jon Sobrino, 'Christian Prayer and New Testament Theology: A Basis for Social Justice and Spirituality', in Matthew Fox (ed.) *Western Spirituality*, Bear and Co., Sante Fe, 1981, p.79.

thought it applies equally to the transformation of society:

> Prayer and meditation have an important part to play in opening up new ways and new horizons. If our prayer is the expression of a deep and grace-inspired desire for newness of life — and not the mere blind attachment to what has always been familiar and 'safe' — God will act in us and through us to renew the Church by preparing, in prayer, what we cannot yet imagine or understand. In this way our prayer and faith today will be orientated toward the future which we ourselves may never see fully realized on earth.[28]

But just as action is blind without prayer and reflection, so prayer negates itself if it does not become action.[29] This has been increasingly discovered in our time by many Christians of different traditions as they have sought to live the Christian life in the world, not least by those who have identified themselves with the struggles of the poor and the oppressed for liberation.[30] Christian spirituality enables Christians to live life within the orbit of God's renewing grace in the midst of participating in the struggle for what is right, good and just in the world. Christian spirituality and participation in those actions consonant with what we know of God's purposes in society belong inseparably together.

The potential power of prayer in relation to social transformation must not be underestimated or misunderstood. That it often is, soon became apparent in the heated debate surrounding the South African Council of Churches' call for a day of prayer on 16 June 1985, for an end to unjust rule.[31] For some such a call was tantamount to treason and, at the very least, an unholy attempt to cajole God into taking politi-

---

[28] Thomas Merton, *Contemplation in a World of Action*, Doubleday, New York, 1973, p.179.

[29] See Karl Barth's discussion of this in his essay 'Church and State' in *Community, State and Church*, Doubleday, New York, 1960, pp.135ff.

[30] For an overview of what characterises this spirituality, see Casiano Floristan, 'Spirituality: A Retrospect and Prospective View', in Paul Brand, Edward Schillebeeckx and Anton Weiler (eds.), *Concilium*, December 1983, pp.53ff.

[31] See 'A Theological Rationale and a Call to Prayer for the End to Unjust Rule' adopted by the South African Council of Churches on 16 April 1985, *Journal of Theology for Southern Africa* no. 52, September 1985.

cal sides or changing his mind. Others thought it meant introducing politics into prayer, as though this had never been done before — which is, of course, nonsense when one recalls that prayer is used to open Parliament, and before military battle. In the light of the gospel there is surely less justification to pray for military victory against one's enemies than there is to pray for an end to injustice.

If the relating of prayer and politics is not new, what is new for many people is that prayer should no longer be harnessed in support of those in power and the maintenance of the status quo, but in the service of the transformation of society. This does not mean that Christians should no longer pray for those in authority, but that they should pray for them on the basis of what the kingdom of God requires of rulers. The priestly, prayerful service which the church renders to the state cannot be separated, as Karl Barth shows, from its prophetic responsibility. Prayer for those in authority is not meant as unequivocal support for all they do: it is also a sign of the limits beyond which the state dare not transgress.[32]

With all this in mind, then, it is not surprising that Karl Barth can speak of the subversive character of spirituality. 'To clasp hands in prayer' he writes, 'is the beginning of an uprising against the disorder of the world.'[33] Similarly Adrian Hastings, in reflecting on the political role of African Independent churches, reminds us that as 'unpolitical as intense prayer may be in intention, the power it provides ensures that it will often not be so in consequence.'[34]

The real difference which divides people on an issue such as the call to pray for the end to unjust rule derives in large measure from one's position in society, and the racial and class interests which relate to that position.[35] The powerful, so it would appear, allow the use of prayer to maintain their

[32] Karl Barth, *op. cit.*

[33] Quoted by Kenneth Leach, *True Prayer: An Introduction to Christian Spirituality,* Anglican Book Centre, Toronto, 1980, p.68.

[34] Adrian Hastings, *A History of African Christianity, 1950-1975,* Cambridge University Press, 1979, p.266.

[35] See my essay 'Christians in Conflict: the Social Reality of the South African Church', *Journal of Theology for Southern Africa,* no. 51, June 1985, pp.16ff.

privilege, but the poor cannot pray to be delivered from evil as they perceive it! But surely true Christian prayer has to be consonant with what is revealed to be God's will in scripture, and nothing is more certain than that God's will is for social justice. To pray for an end to unjust rule is not twisting God's arm to do something he had not previously thought to do; it is placing oneself at his disposal in the struggle for justice. It is by no means unwarranted exegesis to believe that the prayer for an end to injustice in South Africa and elsewhere is consonant with what Jesus taught us to pray: 'deliver us from evil'.

There are, of course, some dangers that need to be avoided here. The first is reducing prayer to a political act. In this essay we have not attempted to examine what is meant by prayer, nor have we paused to consider how prayer may change social reality. This has been discussed fully by others and is beyond the scope of what I am here attempting.[36] Prayer in its various forms, as I understand it, has to do with our relationship with God; it is an essential expression of that relationship. If social and political issues are of importance in our lives, as they should be if we are Christians, then it is both right and natural that they become a matter of prayer.

A second danger is the more general one of developing a spirituality of paternalism or privileged guilt, the spirituality of those who identify with the poor and other victims of society in order to satisfy their own needs and assuage their own guilt. But that is not the spirituality which derives from the gospel which sets us free and enables us to love our neighbour and enemy despite the cost to ourselves. Love always demands a surrender of oneself to another, and 'the surrender to others' writes Sobrino, 'rarely reaches as great a fullness as in the struggle for justice in which the element of gratification may be more lacking than in the other expressions of love'.[37]

---

[36] See Vincent Brummer, *What are we doing when we pray?* SCM, London, 1984, esp. chaps. 5-7.
[37] Jon Sobrino, *op. cit.*, p.97f.

The 'spirituality of liberation' is, however, not simply the spirituality of those who have identified themselves with the struggles of the poor and the oppressed. It is also, perhaps even more, the spirituality of the victims themselves. Gustavo Gutierrez writes of 'the birth of a new spirituality' which, 'eschewing the escapism of purely formal, superficial "prayer and celebration", surges up from the struggles of the poor'. It is not easy, of course, to sing the Lord's song in exile or captivity. But, writes Gutierrez, 'nowhere is the living God sung with more faith, hope, and joy than in the world of the masses'. And, he continues,

> there is, perhaps, nothing more impressive and creative than the prayerful praxis of Christians among the poor and oppressed. Theirs is not a prayer divorced from the liberating praxis of people. On the contrary, the Christian prayer of the poor springs up from the roots of that very practice.[38]

Thus, the spirituality of liberation not only has the potential to transform the perspective of those on top so that they see things as they appear from below and act accordingly, but it also enables those below to see beyond their bondage, gives them courage to break their chains, and awakens hope that cannot be quenched until fulfilled. In this way, writes Matthew Lamb,

> the recovery of the Christian spirituality of social justice offers the possibility of converting the human drama of history away from death toward life. Such spirituality unites the Mystery of God with the mystery of human personhood and reveals the redemptive solidarity of God with the poor and oppressed victims of history.[39]

On the occasion of his godson, Dietrich Bethge's baptism in May 1944, Bonhoeffer wrote a sermon from prison in which he said:

> 'Our church, which has been fighting in these years only

[38] Gustavo Gutierrez, *The Power of the Poor in History*, SCM, London, 1983, p.106.
[39] Matthew Lamb, 'Christian Spirituality and Social Justice', *Horizons* 10/1, 1983, p.32.

for its self-preservation, as though that were an end in itself, is incapable of taking the word of reconciliation and redemption to mankind and the world. Our earlier words are therefore bound to lose their force and cease, and our being Christians today will be limited to two things: prayer and righteous action among men. All Christian thinking, speaking, and organising must be born anew out of this prayer and action.'[40]

That is the heart of Christian spirituality, the spirituality of the kingdom of God and his justice.

Spirituality and the rebirth of culture

In a recent encyclopaedia article we are told that 'every people gives a particular stamp to its own spirituality by virtue of its patterns of thought and its cultural history'.[41] It is possible, for example, to speak of Irish, German or Spanish spirituality; it is also possible to speak of African or Afrikaner spirituality within South Africa. But as yet it is not possible to speak of a South African spirituality, for that would imply the emergence of a common culture and set of values, that is, a common conception and experiencing of the world in which we live. 'A particular type of piety,' Pannenberg observes, 'involves not only a specific theological focus and corresponding life-styles but also a particular conception of the human world, the world of human experience.'[42] If social transformation is to have any lasting significance, and if it is not to result in further unjust social structures, then the spirituality of which we have been speaking must also be related to the rebirth of culture in ways consonant with the kingdom of God.

The relationship between culture and Christianity has always been problematic. The mere fact that Christianity has to be expressed and communicated implies that it has to relate to the culture in which it is present. At the same time,

[40] *Letters and Papers from Prison*, p.300.
[41] Gerhard Wehr, 'German Spirituality', in Gordon S. Wakefield, *The Westminster Dictionary of Christian Spirituality*, Westminster, Philadelphia, 1983, p.169.
[42] Pannenberg, *op. cit.*, p.16.

history is full of evidence that Christian faith can so easily become captive to culture and deny itself. This is as true in South Africa as it has ever been elsewhere, particularly because culture has become a key element in the structuring and legitimation of apartheid.[43] In this way culture has become part of the ideological conflict that divides people and the churches into opposing factions.

Spirituality is not immune from this conflict any more than theology or other dimensions of the life of the church.[44] Undoubtedly the most acute conflict between spiritualities in South Africa today is betweeen those which see piety as unrelated to social change or as sanctifying the given order, and those which relate positively to the spirituality of the kingdom of God I have described. This conflict has little to do with traditional divisions; it has a great deal to do with present group interests, and therefore with the cultural history of South Africa. Social transformation implies, then, the liberation of culture from its misuse, and its rebirth in the creation of a just society and worldview.

European Christianity arrived in South Africa in a variety of forms, each of which had been shaped previously by other cultural experiences in Western Europe. I refer to the Dutch Calvinism and German Lutheranism of the first settlers, and the Roman Catholicism, Anglicanism, Scottish Presbyterianism, and English Free Church traditions of the majority of the missionaries and those who settled in South Africa during the nineteenth century. Smaller and subsequent groups of settlers and missionaries brought with them their own ethnic interpretations of Christianity whether Scandinavian Lutheran, Portuguese Catholic, Greek Orthodox, or North American liberal Protestantism, fundamentalism or Pentecostalism. Each of these traditions has introduced its own distinct form of spirituality into South Africa clothed within the culture of its historical origin. The ways in which each

---

[43] See Buti Thlhagale, 'Culture in an Apartheid Society', *Journal of Theology for Southern Africa*, no. 51, June 1985, p.27f.
[44] See my essay 'Theologies in Conflict: the South African Debate', in Villa-Vicencio and de Gruchy, *Resistance and Hope: South African Essays in Honour of Beyers Naude*, David Philip, Cape Town, Eerdmans, Grand Rapids, 1985.

tradition has reacted to its new historical context have varied a great deal, some being more open and ecumenical and others being more closed and introverted.

There were indigenous cultures flourishing in what is now South Africa prior to the arrival of European Christianity, and these, though varied, were inevitably religious in character. Without romanticising, it remains true that a profound sense of the presence of God is evident in traditional African culture.[45] Tragically this was not recognised by those Europeans, whether settlers or missionaries, who first introduced Christianity to the sub-continent. They regarded the indigenous cultures as devoid of any genuine religious life and belief in God, considering them too primitive to be taken seriously or so demonic that they could only be rejected.[46] Contrary to scripture, according to the missionaries God had left himself without a witness in southern Africa.

Despite the fact that African society has undergone successive cultural shocks during the past three hundred years as a result of its encounter with European colonisation and culture, traditional African spirituality has survived. This is true both within and beyond the churches. According to census figures, whilst most blacks in South Africa are members of a Christian church, about twenty percent of the black population of South Africa still adhere to traditional religion.[47] Moreover, it has been estimated that six million members belong to the various black indigenous churches in South Africa, that is, to churches which have in varying degrees related their Christian faith to traditional spirituality. Although suppressed within the mainline churches, elements of African spirituality and culture have always been present even if sometimes dormant, and in our time a renaissance has begun that is of considerable significance.

At this point more conservative Christians might well fear some form of syncretism, that is, the destruction of Christian

---

[45] A good general introduction is Benjamin C. Ray, *African Religions*, Prentice Hall, New Jersey, 1976.

[46] See Gabriel Setiloane, *The Image of God among the Sotho-Tswana*, Balkema, Rotterdam, 1976.

[47] 1980 Government census.

faith through wedding it with alien elements. This is an anxiety which we must take seriously. There is a core of basic belief which cannot be surrendered without Christianity losing its identity. Moreover, as we have noted already, Christianity can so easily become captive to alien cultures and, in the process, not only lose its distinctive character and witness but also be misused to sanction and legitimate something contrary to the gospel. Christians in South Africa need to be particularly sensitive to this because of the unholy alliance between Christianity and culture evident in the ideology, legitimation and practice of apartheid.

The problem of syncretism is very complex, indeed, the more it is examined the more complex it appears. Many who react most strongly against the dangers of syncretism assume that there is such a thing as 'pure Christianity', that is, Christianity untouched in any way by culture. Generally, they regard their version of Christianity as the criterion by which all others must be judged. The unquestioned conviction that many European missionaries in South Africa had that their Christianity was pure when in fact it was so deeply trapped in European culture, social interests and colonial politics, is a salutary example. Those whites who today level the accusation of syncretism at black Christians need to consider the 'plank in their own eye' before saying too much about 'the mote' in that of their brothers and sisters.[48]

Lesslie Newbigin in *The Other Side of 1984* writes that 'it would be hard to deny that British (and most of western) Christianity is an advanced case of syncretism'. He continues:

> The Church has lived so long as a permitted and privileged minority, accepting relegation to the private sphere in a culture whose public life is controlled by a totally different vision of reality, that it has almost lost the power to address a radical challenge to that vision and therefore to 'modern western civilization' as a whole.[49]

---

[48] See Desmond Tutu, 'Spirituality: Christian and African', in Charles Villa-Vicencio and John W. de Gruchy, *op. cit.*, pp.159f.

[49] Lesslie Newbigin, *The Other Side of 1984*, WCC, Geneva, 1983, p.23.

The fact of the matter is that particularly since the eighteenth century Enlightenment, Western culture has increasingly cut itself adrift from the Christian tradition. Although ideologies have arisen to fill the vacuum, Western culture has become fragmented and disparate, without a common vision or set of values.[50] This has had severe spiritual ramifications, both personal and social, leading amongst other things to the crisis of meaning which is endemic to most European societies. One serious symptom is cynical nihilism, the surrender of hope and therefore moral responsibility. Related to that is a rampant individualism which destroys human community and produces the privatization of piety that not only undermines Christian community but also Christian witness in society. The church must, in large measure, accept responsibility for this inner, spiritual collapse of European culture which reached its nadir in the rise of Nazism but is omnipresent in secularism.[51]

There is, on the contrary, a great deal in African traditional culture which is far more consonant with the biblical tradition.[52] Itumeleng Mosala concludes his article on 'African Traditional Beliefs and Christianity' by saying:

> whereas Christianity would need to be subjected to thorough purification and de-ideologisation before its relationship with African religion can be properly established, there is nevertheless a striking and fruitful relation between the *biblical communities* as we encounter them in scripture and African religion.[53]

In rejecting syncretism there is, then, a danger that we regard all cultures and ideologies in an undifferentiated way. Cultures and ideologies vary a great deal, some being far more consonant with Christian faith than others, and others being blatantly destructive of the gospel.

---

[50] See, for example, Alasdair MacIntyre, *After Virtue*, Notre Dame, Indiana, 1981.

[51] See Dietrich Bonhoeffer's essay, 'Inheritance and Decay' in *Ethics*, Macmillan, New York, 1965, pp.88ff.

[52] See Kwesi Dickson and Paul Ellingworth, *Biblical Revelation and African Beliefs*, Orbis, Maryknoll NY., 1969.

[53] *Journal of Theology for Southern Africa*, no. 43, June 1983, p.24.

In struggling for social justice in South Africa the church is also called to strive for the renewal of culture in ways consonant with the values of the kingdom of God. This does not mean Christian triumphalism any more than it requires an end to cultural diversity, a cultural reductionism. It means overcoming the apartheid abuse of culture, discovering and affirming all that is consonant with the vision of the kingdom of God in each culture, whether African or European, and moving beyond the static petrification of our respective cultural inheritances. This means enabling the rebirth of culture so that it is no longer a dehumanizing mill-stone around the neck of South Africa but a vehicle for a new society of justice, freedom and human dignity. Tlhagale speaks to this imperative when he says:

> If our traditional perception of culture retains and easily perpetuates traditionalism and the conflicts endemic in society then a new conception of culture becomes imperative. Culture need not just be a reflection of a social heritage, nor a means whereby class structures or class interests are reproduced. . . . The expectation is that culture, understood in its utopian dimension, would allow for freedom and creativity, that it would enable man to continuously strive for the humanization of man in community.[54]

Social transformation in South Africa does not simply mean an end to apartheid and injustice, it means the birth of a culture which points in the direction of the kingdom of God. And that is a profoundly spiritual matter.

Keeping hope alive

For many white South Africans the envisioned utopia of the apartheid-dream is being replaced by a nightmare of fears and a spirit of apprehensiveness. The idealism which marked the early devotees of the ideology has turned sour

---

[54] Buti Tlhagale, *op. cit.*, p.33.

and produced widespread cynicism. The vision has proved empty and beyond realisation. The emergence of a spirit of cynicism is a sign that a society and its culture has become sick unto death. Without the birth of hope there can be no future, but hope is not shallow optimism, it is something born out of the struggle for what is right and just.

Shortly before his arrest, and amidst the growing awareness that Nazi Germany was doomed, Dietrich Bonhoeffer wrote the following:

> It is true that there is a silly, cowardly kind of optimism, which we must condemn. But the optimism that is will for the future should never be despised, even if it is proved wrong a hundred times; it is health and vitality, and the sick man has no business to impugn it. There are people who regard it as frivolous, as some Christians think it impious for anyone to hope and prepare for a better earthly future. They think that the meaning of present events is chaos, disorder and catastrophe; and in resignation or pious escapism they surrender all responsibility for reconstruction and for future generations. It may be that the day of judgment will dawn tomorrow; in that case, we will gladly stop working for a better future. But not before.[55]

Cynical resignation is a deadly sin, it destroys hope and with it any sense of responsibility, any genuine love or faith, any commitment to the struggle for justice. It is the antithesis of the fruit of genuine Christian spirituality.

On reflection, the fruit of Christian spirituality which Paul sums up as 'faith, hope, and love' has a special pertinence in the struggle for justice. Unbelief is clinging to false gods in the hope that they will bring security. White South Africans, along with the privileged in every country, have placed their hope far too much in their race, wealth and military might, and far too little in the God of righteousness and justice. When these idols crash to the ground, as they always have in the past and must in the future, fear, anxiety and despair

---

[55] *Letters and Papers from Prison, op. cit.,* p.15.

result. Unless this in turn leads to repentance and change, a genuine seeking after God, it results in flight. For those who can afford it, flight from the country; for those who cannot, flight into the laager of self-righteousness and self-defence with its cynical disregard of the cry for justice and the biblical injunction to love one's neighbour and even one's enemy.

Yet there is, despite everything, an amazing sense of hope amongst many South Africans, even amongst those whose present struggle seems so hopeless. It is also a hope that is increasingly embracing both white and black, a hope that really does believe that justice will ultimately triumph, that genuine rather than bogus peace is possible, and that a new society will be born in which all South Africans will be at home. This hoping against hope is very much part of kingdom spirituality. It is an acknowledgement that injustice is contrary to God's will, and a trust that God's purposes of shalom are being worked out in history. It is also a commitment to work for change, to participate in the birth of the new society despite the pain that must accompany it, and therefore it is a rejection of cynical disregard for future generations and an expression of confidence in the God of justice and peace. This hope is the transforming dynamic of Christian spirituality.

1

The God of our Ancestors

The Christian life is rooted in the historical pilgrimage of the people of God. A profound sense of belonging to a community of faith which stretches back into the distant past, and an awareness of being presently 'surrounded by a great cloud of witnesses', is an essential part of both biblical and African tradition.

I Am who I Am

Exodus 3:13-15 (JB)

Moses said to God, 'I am to go, then, to the sons of Israel and say to them, "The God of your fathers has sent me to you". But if they ask me what his name is, what am I to tell them?' And God said to Moses, 'I Am who I Am. This,' he added 'is what you must say to the sons of Israel: "I Am has sent me to you".' And God also said to Moses. 'You are to say to the sons of Israel: "Yahweh, the God of your fathers, the God of Abraham, the God of Isaac, and the God of Jacob, has sent me to you". This is my name for all time; by this name I shall be invoked for all generations to come.'

The God of our ancestors

The Good News for Ethiopia

Acts 8:27-35 (JB)

Ethiopia is the symbol of African independence, and of African Christianity untainted by European culture. Christianity was an African religion centuries before it penetrated Europe.

Now it happened that an Ethiopian had been on pilgrimage to Jerusalem; he was a eunuch and an officer at the court of the kandake, or queen of Ethiopia, and was in fact her chief treasurer. He was now on his way home; and as he sat in his chariot he was reading the prophet Isaiah. The Spirit said to Philip, 'Go up and meet that chariot'. When Philip ran up, he heard him reading Isaiah the prophet and asked, 'Do you understand what you are reading?' 'How can I' he replied 'unless I have someone to guide me?' So he invited Philip to get in and sit by his side. Now the passage of scripture he was reading was this:

Like a sheep that is led to the slaughter-house,
like a lamb that is dumb in front of its shearers,
like these he never opens his mouth.
He has been humiliated and has no one to defend him.
Who will ever talk about his descendants,
since his life on earth has been cut short?

The eunuch turned to Philip and said, 'Tell me, is the prophet referring to himself or someone else?' Starting, therefore, with this text of scripture Philip proceeded to explain the Good News of Jesus to him.

I am an African

Gabriel Setiloane[1]

They call me an African
African indeed am I:
Rugged son of the soil of Africa,
Black as my father, and his before him;
As my mother and sisters and brothers, living
and gone from this world.

---

[1] Gabriel Setiloane is a Methodist theologian and pastor. He is presently an Associate Professor in the Department of Religious Studies at the University of Cape Town. 'I am an African' was first published in *Risk*, WCC, IX/3, 1973.

They ask me what I believe . . . my faith.
Some even think I have none
But live like the beasts of the field.

'What of God, the Creator
Revealed to mankind through the Jews of old,
the YAHWEH: I AM
Who has been and ever shall be?
Do you acknowledge him?'

My fathers and theirs, many generations before, knew Him.
They bowed the knee to Him
By many names they knew Him,
And yet 'tis He the One and only God
They called Him
UVELINGQAKI:
The first One
Who came ere ever anything appeared:
UNKULUNKULU:
The BIG BIG ONE,
So big indeed that no space could ever contain Him.
MODIMO:
Because His abode is far up in the sky.
They also knew Him as MODIRI:
For He has made all:
and LESA:
The spirit without which the breath of man cannot be.

But, my fathers, from the mouths of their fathers, say
That this God of old shone
With a brightness so bright
It blinded them. . . . Therefore. . . .
He died himself, UVELINGQAKI,
That none should reach His presence. . . .
Unless they die (for pity flowed in His heart).
Only the fathers who are dead come into His presence.

Little gods bearing up the prayers and supplications
Of their children to the GREAT GOD. . . .
'Tell us further you African:
What of Jesus, the Christ,

Born in Bethlehem:
Son of Man and Son of God
Do you believe in Him?'

For ages He eluded us, this Jesus of Bethlehem, Son of Man:
Going first to Asia and to Europe, and the western sphere,
Some say He tried to come to us,
Sending His messengers of old. . . . But. . . .
They were cut off by the desert and the great mountains of
     Ethiopia!'
Wanderers from behind those mountains have told
Strange tales to our fathers,
And they in turn to others.

Tales of the Man of Bethlehem
Who went about doing good!
The theme of His truths is now lost in the mouths of women
As they sissed their little children and themselves to sleep.

Later on, He came, this Son of Man:
Like a child delayed He came to us.
The White Man brought Him.
He was pale, and not the Sunburnt Son of the Desert.
As a child He came.

A wee little babe wrapped in swaddling clothes.
Ah, if only He had been like little Moses lying
Sun-scorched on the banks of the River of God
We would have recognized Him.
He eludes us still this Jesus, Son of Man.

His words. Ah, they taste so good
As sweet and refreshing as the sap of the palm raised and
     nourished on African soil
The Truths of His words are for all men, for all time.

And yet for us it is when He is on the cross,
This Jesus of Nazareth, with holed hands
and open side, like a beast at a sacrifice:
When He is stripped naked like us,
Browned and sweating water and blood in the heat of the sun,

Yet silent,
That we cannot resist Him.

How like us He is, this Jesus of Nazareth,
Beaten, tortured, imprisoned, spat upon, truncheoned,
Denied by His own, and chased like a thief in the night.
Despised, and rejected like a dog that has fleas, for
    NO REASON.

No reason, but that He was Son of his Father,
OR . . . was there a reason?
There was indeed . . .
As in that sheep or goat we offer in sacrifice,
Quiet and uncomplaining.
Its blood falling to the ground to cleanse it, as us:
And making peace between us and our fathers long passed
    away.
He is that LAMB!
His blood cleanses,
not only us,
not only the clan,
not only the tribe,
But all, all MANKIND:
Black and White and Brown and Red,
All Mankind!

HO! . . . Jesus, Lord, Son of Man and Son of God,
Make peace with your blood and sweat and suffering,
With God, UVELINGQAKI, UNKULUNKULU,
For the sins of Mankind, our fathers and us,
That standing in the same Sonship with all mankind and you,
Together with you, we can pray to Him above:
FATHER FORGIVE.

Faithful through all generations
Psalm 100

O shout to the Lord in triumph, all the earth:
serve the Lord with gladness,
and come before his face with songs of joy.

Know that the Lord he is God:

it is he who has made us and we are his;
we are his people and the sheep of his pasture.

Come into his gates with thanksgiving,
and into his courts with praise:
give thanks to him, and bless his holy name.

For the Lord is good, his loving mercy is for ever:
his faithfulness throughout all generations.

A prayer for Africa

This prayer is used at the end of the liturgy in some churches in South Africa. It may be used at the conclusion of each of the sets of readings which follow.

God bless Africa,
guard her peoples
guide her rulers
and grant her peace.   Amen.

Our Refuge and Redeemer

The Christian life is lived in awareness of God as the creator and ultimate reality which enfolds us, the one 'in whom we live, move and have our being'. An early North African theologian, St Augustine, reminds us that God 'made us for himself, and our hearts are restless till they rest in him'. The creator who is 'our refuge' has revealed himself in Jesus Christ as 'our redeemer'. The Christian life expresses its praise and gratitude to God the creator and redeemer in 'psalms, hymns and spiritual songs'. One of the greatest gifts which African Christianity offers the universal church is the beauty, richness, harmony and spontaneity of its song.

Before the mountains were born

Psalm 90:1-2

Lord, you have been our refuge:
from one generation to another.

Before the mountains were born
or the earth and the world were brought to be:
from eternity to eternity you are God.

Be still and know that I am God

Psalm 46

God is our refuge and strength:
a very present help in trouble.

Therefore we will not fear, though the earth be moved:
and though the mountains are shaken
in the midst of the sea;

Though the waters rage and foam:
and though the mountains quake at the rising of the sea.

There is a river whose streams make glad the city of God:
the holy dwelling-place of the Most High.

God is in the midst of her,
therefore she shall not be moved:
God will help her, and at break of day.

The nations make uproar, and the kingdoms are shaken:
but God has lifted his voice, and the earth shall tremble.

The Lord of hosts is with us:
The God of Jacob is our stronghold.

Come then and see what the Lord has done:
what destruction he has brought upon the earth.

He makes wars to cease in all the world:
he breaks the bow and shatters the spear,
and burns the chariots in the fire.

'Be still, and know that I am God:
I will be exalted among the nations,
I will be exalted upon the earth.'

The Lord of hosts is with us:
The God of Jacob is our stronghold.

Worship in Spirit and truth   John 4:19-24 (NIV)

'Sir,' the woman said, 'I can see that you are a prophet. Our fathers worshipped on this mountain, but you Jews claim that the place where we must worship is in Jerusalem.' Jesus declared, 'Believe me, woman, a time is coming when you will worship the Father neither on this mountain nor in Jerusalem. You Samaritans worship what you do not know; we worship what we do know, for salvation is from the Jews. Yet a time is coming and has now come when the true worshippers will worship the Father in spirit and in truth, for they are the kind of worshippers the Father seeks. God is spirit, and his worshippers must worship in spirit and in truth. The woman said, 'I know that Messiah' (called Christ) 'is coming. When he comes, he will explain everything to us.' Then Jesus declared, 'I who speak to you am he.'

Ntsikana the witness

Jeff Opland[2]

Ntsikana (c. 1780-1821) is linked with the beginnings of Christianity among the Xhosa-speaking people. He is revered by many Africans as a prophet and a saint. His Great Hymn can be regarded as the beginnings of an indigenous theology in southern Africa.[3]

Ntsikana might have heard the preaching of the missionary Johannes van der Kemp at the end of the eighteenth century; certainly Ntsikana associated himself with Williams' Kat River mission station. After the death of Williams he tried to lead his followers to Brownlee's new mission station in the Tyhume Valley, but he died before he reached Gwali, probably in 1821.[4] At some indeterminate time, Ntsikana had a conversion experience that led him to abjure certain traditional customs. He gathered about him a band of disciples who met for regular worship that included some songs and a hymn of his own composition. Makaphela Noyi Balfour, the son of Ntsikana's principle disciple and successor, described Ntsikana's services as follows:

> At divine service he used to sit near the doorway, while the rest of the hut was filled completely with people, men and women. His kaross of male leopard skins covered his body entirely, that body he would not reveal even to himself. The prelude to the service was the hymn *That Great Cloak that Covereth Us*. And when his disciples had thus acknowledged his entry, he would then preach this thing

[2] Jeff Opland, *Xhosa Oral Poetry*, Ravan Press, Johannesburg, 1984, pp.212-3.
[3] Janet Hodgson, *Ntsikana's Great Hymn: A Xhosa Expression of Christianity in the early 19th Century Eastern Cape*, Centre.for African Studies, University of Cape Town, 1980, p.1.
[4] Johannes van der Kemp, Joseph Williams and John Brownlee were missionaries of the London Missionary Society. See Jane Sales, *Mission Stations and the Coloured Communities of the Eastern Cape, 1800-1852*, Balkema, Cape Town, 1975.

that had entered him, this thing that hated sin. And he would name what was sinful in their daily lives, pointing out whatever in them was hateful to God. . . . This man preached Christ, saying, 'Repent ye! Repent ye from your sins!' He preached the Son of God, the only begotten of His Father, the Great Cloak, the true Refuge, the Stronghold and Rock of Truth.

The Great Blanket with which we are clothed

Ntsikana's Great Hymn

There have been several English translations of Ntsikana's hymn since it was first composed in Xhosa around 1820. The translation used here has been specially prepared for this volume by Fr. Dave Dargie of Lumko Institute so that it can be sung to the traditional tune. The hymn begins with 'Ntsikana's Bell'. The pealing of the bells (Ahom, Ahom!) calls the people to worship.

a. Ntsikana's Bell

Sele! Sele! Ahom, ahom ahom!
Come forward, come forward,
Our creator God is calling.
Ahom, ahom, ahom, ahom, ahom!

b. (Solo) uDal'ubom

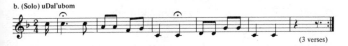

(3 verses)

Behold — behold the Life-Creator,
dwelling in the highest.

Behold — behold the Life-Creator,
it is He who calls us.
Behold — behold the Life-Creator,
let us call together.

All: Ahom, ahom, ahom, ahom, ahom!

c. Great Hymn

Ele le le homna, hom, homna
Ele le le homna, hom, homna
Ele le le homna, hom, homna

Verses

It is you are the Great God, who dwells on high,
It is you, it is you, true shield, protector,
It is you, it is you, true fortress, stronghold,
It is you, it is you, true forest of refuge,
It is you, it is you, true rock of power,
It is you, it is you, who dwells in the highest.

You Life-Creator, created on high
You, the Creator who created the skies,
The Maker of stars, the Pleiades you made.
A Star flashed upon us, bearing your message,
You made even the blind for your good purpose.

The trumpet has sounded, it too has called us,
It is you, the hunter, who hunts us to save us,
You gather together flocks rejecting each other.

It is you, our leader, it is you who lead us,
You are the Great Blanket with which we are clothed.

Ahom, homna! Your hands are wounded,
Ahom, homna! Your feet are wounded,
Ahom! Your life-blood — why is it streaming?
Ahom! Your life-blood — was shed for us.
Ahom! Are we worthy — of such a ransom?
Ahom! Are we worthy — to enter your homestead?
Ahom, Little Lamb — you are Messiah.

Ele le le homna, hom! Homna!
Ele le le homna, hom! Homna!
Ele le le homna, hom! Homna!

The God of the Nations

The Christian life is lived in the midst of the world and not in a separate ghetto untouched by the struggles and pains, the guilt and the failures, the fears and the hopes of the nation. Yet even in the land of your birth you can be an exile and an alien, a 'stranger and pilgrim', crying out to God for a new day in which a new song can be sung.

How can we sing the Lord's song? Psalm 137

By the waters of Babylon we sat down and wept:
when we remembered Zion.

As for our harps we hung them up:
upon trees that are in that land.

For there those who led us away captive
required of us a song:
and those who had despoiled us demanded mirth,
saying 'Sing us one of the songs of Zion.'

How can we sing the Lord's song in a strange land?

Sing a new song Psalm 96

O sing to the Lord a new song:
sing to the Lord, all the earth.

Sing to the Lord and bless his holy name:
proclaim the good news of his salvation from day to day.

Declare his glory among the nations:
and his wonders among all peoples.

For great is the Lord, and greatly to be praised:
he is more to be feared than all gods.

As for all the gods of the nations, they are mere idols:
it is the Lord who made the heavens.

Majesty and glory are before him:
beauty and power are in his sanctuary.

Render to the Lord, you families of the nations:
render to the Lord glory and might.

Render to the Lord the honour due to his name:
bring offerings and come into his courts.

O worship the Lord in the beauty of holiness:
let the whole earth stand in awe of him.

Say among the nations that the Lord is king:
he has made the world so firm that it can never be moved;
and he shall judge the peoples with equity.

Let the heavens rejoice and let the earth be glad:
let the sea roar, and all that fills it.

Let the fields rejoice, and everything in them:
then shall all the trees of the wood
shout for joy before the Lord;

For he comes, he comes to judge the earth:
he shall judge the world with righteousness,
and the peoples with his truth.

On anthems and idols John de Gruchy

Christians are citizens of two kingdoms. Our ultimate loyalty is to the God of the nations, not to any particular nation. We are most patriotic when we love our country so much that we refuse to allow it to become absolute in our lives. We accept its guilt and failures as our own, but we refuse to accept things which are wrong and unjust. We are prepared to be ostracised by society for the sake of society. Our loyalty to the God of the nations makes us deeply concerned that our country should exhibit that righteousness which alone exhalts a nation (Proverbs 14:34). In seeking to be true patriots, Christians have seldom been popular. Like Jeremiah the prophet they have even been called traitors (see especially Jeremiah chaps. 28 and 37).

Every nation develops symbols, such as national anthems, which unite it in a common purpose. These symbols are important and can enable a nation to flourish justly and wisely, drawing on its collective experience through the centuries. The danger is that sometimes these very symbols become idols designed to glorify the nation and justify its deeds whether right or wrong, or that the symbols themselves become substitutes for reality.

Many nations have regarded themselves as specially chosen, not to serve but to rule. Many nations have believed in a manifest destiny that gave them special rights over others. Patriotism thus becomes individual selfishness writ large; it is group egoism. National symbols have given powerful, emotive expression to this conviction. When this happens it makes the nation an end in itself demanding absolute loyalty. This the Christian cannot give, for absolute loyalty belongs to God alone. The true calling which God gives to any nation is a vocation to serve others; the only anthem that should be sung is that which glorifies the creator who is the king, redeemer and judge of all nations.

South Africa is regarded by some as a country of many nations, by others as a nation made up of different cultures struggling to become one nation. The latter is the vision that inspires many of us. It recognises the rich diversity of tongue and custom, but it abhors the divisions which separate people because of race and class so that they become enemies of each other, unknown to one another in their own, common land. There is a deep love for South Africa amongst all groups who inhabit it, but there is also a deep divide, a bitter wall of partition and alienation which frustrates the discovery of each other as human beings bound to a common land and destiny. It is difficult to sing a common song of praise in such an estranged land.

The present national anthem of South Africa, *Die Stem*, means a great deal to many whites, especially Afrikaners. It arose out of the latter's struggle against British imperialism and as an expression of identity and patriotism. For others, however, especially black but also white South Africans, it is a sectional anthem now identified with an ideology of separation. It has become divisive and can no longer be sung. For many of us it exalts the nation in a way that runs contrary to the gospel of Jesus Christ, for the gospel calls us to follow Christ even unto death, but the anthem calls us to live and die for South Africa.

It was an Afrikaner, Justice H.A. Fagan, on returning from a great gathering of Africans earlier this century at which the African anthem *Nkosi Sikelel' iAfrika* was sung, who uttered a cry from the heart that needs to be heard today.[5] The words but not the sentiments are dated.

> From lips of thousands swells the music. Ah!
> I close my eyes, and like a seraph choir
> I hear these voices that my soul inspire:
> *Nkosi Sikelel' iAfrika.*
> For Africa we crave Thy blessing, Lord.
> I look, and lo! The Zulu thousands stand,
> Xhosa, Shangaan and Sotho hand in hand,
> And I, a whiteman — bound in one great cord.
> We many races seek the one reward,
> Blessing on one dear home, one fatherland;
> Rooted and grounded here at thy command,
> By one and all Thy blessing be implored!
> We many raise one song, one 'Gloria' —
> *Nkosi Sikelel' iAfrika.*

Whites who see blacks as a threat, who regard black movements struggling for human rights and dignity with fear and

---

[5] The original Afrikaans version was translated into English by Edgar H. Brookes. It was quoted by A.W. Blaxall in 'Even So Send I You', the closing address given at the Rosettenville Conference, July 1949, on *The Christian Citizen in a Multi-Racial South Africa*, Christian Council of South Africa, Strand n.d.

apprehension, will find it difficult to sing *Nkosi Sikelel' iAfrika* because for them it is associated with black resistance to their privileged place. But consider the words, they are not words of hatred, they are not words that evoke violence, they are not words that make nationalism whether black or white an absolute. They are words which seek the blessing of God, that call upon the Spirit to bless all nations of Africa. These are not the words of triumphalism, of haughty pride, but of openness to the Spirit. They represent the cry of hope of exiles in their own land. Surely it is the prayer that should be on all lips who love this land? 'O sing a new song to the Lord all the earth.'

Nkosi Sikele' iAfrika Enoch Sontonga

Nkosi Sikele' iAfrika *is regarded by many blacks and some whites as the national anthem of South Africa. Composed by a teacher, Enoch Sontonga, in a Methodist Mission School at Klipspruit, a town eleven miles west of Johannesburg in 1897, it was first sung at the ordination of a black Methodist minister, the Rev. M. Boweni in 1899. In the words of D.D.T. Jabavu: 'The composition was inspired by a depressed heart, and the refrain testifies to a somewhat melancholy strain.'[6] Soon after the founding of the African National Congress in 1912* Nkosi Sikele' iAfrika *was adopted as its anthem. It is widely sung today, especially at mass rallies of people opposed to apartheid or in non-racial and black churches, and notably at funeral services. We have printed the original Xhosa version, together with an English translation by Fr. Dave Dargie, and a Sotho version and translation, and a Zulu ending.*

---

[6] Lovedale Sol-fa Leaflets, no. 17, 1934.

Xhosa (original version)

Nkosi, sikelel' iAfrika, Maluphakam' uphondo lwayo:
Yiva imithandazo yethu,
Usisikelele, Thina lusapho lwakho.*(twice)*

Yihla Moya, Yihla Moya, Yihla Moya Oyingcwele,
Usisikelele, Thina lusapho lwakho. *(twice)*

English (fits Xhosa tune)
Lord, in your mercy bless Africa,
Lift up the horn of her power and strength.
In your love and kindness hear our prayer,
Father, look on us, and bless your family.

Come, Spirit, come — come and bless us
Come, Spirit, come — come and bless us
Father, look down, and bless Africa,
Father, look on us, and bless your family.

Sotho

Morena boloka sechaba sa heso
O felise lintoa le matšoenyeho. *(twice)*

U se boloke, u se boloke,
U se boloke Morena, u se boloke
Sechaba sa heso, sechaba sa heso. *(twice)*

This ending was composed spontaneously during a meeting.

Zulu

Makube njalo, makube njalo,
Kuze kube ngonaphakade, kuze kube ngonaphakade. *(twice)*

May it be so always,
for ever and ever.

4

God with Us

The Christian life is lived in the world. Christian faith rejects the norms and values of the world, but it affirms that this is the world God created, the world in which God became incarnate in Jesus Christ, the world God loves and seeks to redeem. The biblical tradition rejects any radical separation of the spiritual and material, soul and body; it affirms the wholeness of life and the 'resurrection of the body'. Jesus Christ is God with us, Immanuel, in the flesh.

The Word became flesh

John 1:1-5, 10-14 (NIV)

In the beginning was the Word, and the Word was with God, and the Word was God. He was with God in the beginning. Through him all things were made; without him nothing was made that has been made. In him was life, and that life was the light of men. The light shines in the darkness, but the darkness has not understood it.

He was in the world, and though the world was made through him, the world did not recognise him. He came to that which was his own, but his own did not receive him. Yet to all who received him, to those who believed in his name, he gave the right to become children of God — children born not of natural descent, nor of human decision or a husband's will, but born of God.

The Word became flesh and lived for a while amongst us. We have seen his glory, the glory of the one and only Son, who came from the Father, full of grace and truth.

Immanuel

Matthew 1:22-23 (NIV)

All this took place to fulfil what the Lord had said through the prophet. 'The virgin will be with child and will give birth to a son, and they will call him Immanuel' — which means, 'God with us'.

The Black Madonna

Maria Mackay, OP[7]

Soweto sprawls beneath the stars
While Herod sleeps
Although they're late, the hours he keeps
In curfew'd caution
And, warned in dreams of other roads
I never told him
That I had found the Infant Christ. . . .
Black arms enfold Him.
What, black? What notion?
The dust had settled, satin-soft
On dongas, quilted
Above the little shoe-box house
The Star had halted.
I came from far, I know, a trembling stranger
But might I not approach and touch
that holy manger?

O Woman! You whose lips are rich
Whose breasts are luscious
Would you refuse my starving soul
This gift so precious?
This black-skinned bundle
This Christ to fondle?
She held him close, she held him fast
A continent in cradle
The cloud by day, the fire by night
The Truth behind the Fable
Before the dawn, the winds grew wild

---

[7] Maria Mackay OP, 'The Black Madonna', published in *Grace and Truth*, no. 1, 1983, p.38f.

The seething dust unfurled.
But, the night I came upon her
She held the child
She held the World
That Black Madonna.

Magnificat

Matthew 1:46-55 (JB)

Mary said:
   My soul proclaims the greatness of the Lord
   and my spirit exults in God my saviour;
   because he has looked upon his lowly handmaid.
   Yes, from this day forward all generations
   shall call me blessed,
   for the Almighty has done great things for me.
   Holy is his name,
   and his mercy reaches from age to age for
   those who fear him.
   He has shown the power of his arm,
   he has routed the proud of heart.
   He has pulled down princes from their thrones
   and exalted the lowly.
   The hungry he has filled with good things,
   the rich sent empty away.
   He has come to the help of Israel his servant,
   mindful of his mercy
   — according to the promise he made
   to our ancestors —
   of his mercy to Abraham and to his descendants
   for ever.

God's option for the poor

Frank Chikane[8]

Listen, my dear brothers: it was those who are poor according to the world that God chose, to be rich in faith and to be

---

[8] An edited abstract from Frank Chikane, 'The Incarnation in the Life of the People of Southern Africa', in *The Journal of Theology for Southern Africa*, no. 51, June 1985, p.46f. The Revd. Frank Chikane is a minister of the Apostolic Faith Mission and General Secretary of the Institute for Contextual Theology.

heirs to the kingdom which he promised to those who love him (James 2:5, JB).

Incarnation means identifying with humanity. It means identifying with humanity's weakness, suffering and pain. It means identifying with the struggles of people. That God was made flesh and dwelt amongst us, God amongst the people, God with people; this defies and denies everything in this world's system of values.

The problem today is that Jesus is spoken about in terms and values that are totally alien to him. Jesus is associated today with all the things he denounced and rejected. He is associated with kings and lords, with the powerful and the 'important' people in society, the rich, the oppressors, the exploiters. He is seen as a friend of the upper classes. This must be Jesus the collaborator. It is an image of Jesus created by the powerful as a religious justification for their evil and unjust systems.

If we understand incarnation in terms of the life and attitudes of the historical Jesus then it must be clear that incarnation means making a preferential option for the victims and against the victimiser. Did not the historical Jesus choose to identify and live with the poor, the blind, the sick, and the hungry, thus deliberately associating with a particular class of people in that society? Did not the historical Jesus refuse to be made a king? Did he not rebuke the Pharisees, the chief priests and the scribes? Did he not say to the rich, 'It is easier for a camel to go through the eye of a needle than for a rich man to enter the kingdom of God' (Mark 10:25)? Did he not die the death of a criminal after being sentenced for high treason at the hands of the church leadership and political rulers?

For Jesus there was no question of neutrality in the face of evil and injustices. In the light of the incarnate life of our Lord we are called to abandon false ideas of neutrality, unity and reconciliation. Neutrality in the face of gross injustices, in the face of oppression, domination and exploitation of millions of people, in the face of the violation of human life and integrity is tantamount to collaboration with the forces of evil. We must begin to understand that there is no possibility of unity or reconciliation between the oppressed and the oppressor, the exploiter and the exploited, between good and evil, God and the Devil, without repentance and commitment to the truth.

God's answer to the rich

James 5:1-6 (JB)

Now an answer for the rich. Start crying, weep for the miseries that are coming to you. Your wealth is all rotting, your clothes are all eaten up by moths. All your gold and your silver are corroding away, and the same corrosion will be your own sentence, and eat into your body. It was a burning fire that you stored up as your treasure for the last days. Labourers mowed your fields, and you cheated them — listen to the wages that you kept back, calling out; realise that the cries of the reapers have reached the ears of the Lord of hosts. On earth you have had a life of comfort and luxury; in the time of slaughter you went on eating to your heart's content. It was you who condemned the innocent and killed them; they offered you no resistance.

Lord Jesus, where are you?[9]

What I see in Egoli[10]
are tall buildings
smart cars
well dressed people
a whole scene
that has no place for me
       no place for my wife
no place for my children.

Lord Jesus, where are you?
Are you in those smart white offices
       those smart white houses
       those smart white churches?

[9] An anonymous poem published in *SUCA News*, May 1984, p.14.
[10] Egoli: Johannesburg, the city of gold.

They think you are.
They talk about you the whole time
just as if you were right there with them.
They are so sure
that you are guiding them,
that they are doing your will.
I like to think
that you are actually here with us
that you are one of the left-out ones.

If that is how it is
if you are really here
with us, for us,
I think I could bear it
because I'd know
this wasn't the end,
that you still come
to get prisoners out of gaol
and blind people out of darkness,
to get hungry people into the place
where they can feed their little ones
instead of helplessly hopelessly
listening to them cry.

But my son does not call you Lord,
Jesus,
let alone call on you,
Lord Jesus,
He uses your name as a swearword.
Jesus! he says,
Bloody white man's Jesus!

I fear for him,
for us,
for those whites.

O Jesus, Jesus,
come soon,
clear up the barriers
open it all up, because if you don't
something awful is going to happen.

Do you hear me,
one of those 'homeland' blacks
on the outside looking in?
RSVP
soon.

5

Jesus the True Human

The Christian life means becoming fully human. It is the restoration of God's image in us, the image of the 'Word become flesh', Jesus Christ 'who has been tempted in every way, just as we are — yet was without sin'.

The humanity of Jesus
John 11:32-36 (NIV)

When Mary reached the place where Jesus was and saw him, she fell at his feet and said, 'Lord, if you had been here, my brother would not have died.' When Jesus saw her weeping, and the Jews who had come along with her also weeping, he was deeply moved in spirit and troubled. 'Where have you laid him?' he asked. 'Come and see, Lord,' they replied. Jesus wept. Then the Jews said, 'See how he loved him!'

He made himself nothing
Philippians 2:5-8 (NIV)

Your attitude should be the same as that of Christ Jesus:

Who, being in very nature God,
did not consider equality with God
something to be grasped,
but made himself nothing,
taking the very nature of a servant,
being made in human likeness.

And being found in appearance as a man,
he humbled himself and became obedient to death —
even death on a cross!

The pattern of human dignity and freedom   Siqgibo Dwane[11]

The rediscovery of the manhood of Jesus is accompanied by the realisation that he was poor, and kept humble company. This has been obscured by the institutionalised Christ who is identified with the culture and concerns of the middle and upper class in Western society. Jesus the homeless and defenceless man stands where the poor stand and speaks to the lowly and oppressed, not from outside or above, but from within. The wonder of his life is that in and through him, God, who is eternally secure, exposed himself to the full range of human misery.

St Paul makes reference to the self-emptying of the One who left the riches of his glory and took the form of a servant. This is God, who makes his appearance not in golden apparel for the amusement and delight of rich suburbanites, but in poverty and weakness, in order that they may be appalled and moved to repentance. This is the significance of the story of the rich young man who came to Jesus. People whose aim in life is to accumulate wealth will always find the company of Jesus unbearable. 'How hard it is for a rich man to enter the kingdom of God.' So the rich young man went away sorrowful for he had made the ultimate refusal.

When we say that Jesus is the Son of God, we mean that God himself became the companion of the fishermen of Galilee, of tax collectors like Matthew, and of notorious sinners like Mary Magdalene. God knows the worst excesses of squalor and degradation, not by seeing them through a telescope, but on account of his own baptism in them.

What makes the life of the Man from Nazareth redemptive is that it is God who suffers with him as one of the outcasts and oppressed. This man would not let his spirit be twisted

[11] From Siqgibo Dwane, 'Christology and the Third World,' *Journal of Theology for Southern Africa*, no. 21, December 1977, pp.8-10. Dr. Dwane is Bishop of the Order of Ethiopia within the Anglican Church of the Province of Southern Africa.

and his humanity distorted by hatred of those who inflicted suffering upon him. In him there is found the freedom with which man is endowed at creation, the freedom to be available to God, and to be lined up on his side against the powers of evil, corruption, injustice, greed and ignorance. Jesus as the new Adam is free to be man in God's image because he renounces all self-seeking in order to affirm that the ultimate goal of his existence is to accomplish the purposes of God.

In his triple renunciation of the Tempter's offers Jesus succeeds in upholding and strengthening this freedom to be what by God's design he already is. True manhood is held as a sacred trust from God and receives its mandate from him alone. Jesus therefore refuses to have his mission in the world, and the tools with which to accomplish it, prescribed by anyone other than God. To succumb to the Tempter would have been not only disloyal to God, but also a denial of his humanity. Jesus is therefore the pattern of human dignity and freedom.

Jesus Christ is man liberated from the power of sin which destroys human dignity and defaces the beauty of creation. He is free to be completely available to God, and therefore the powers of destruction hold no sway over him. Instead, he disarmed them and led a host of captives out of captivity. Liberation in the New Testament is prefigured and anticipated in the deliverance of Hebrew slaves from captivity to Pharoah. In biblical terms it is not meant to be interpreted in a narrow, individualistic fashion, but as a comprehensive work which accomplishes the setting free of God's people from powers that are not of divine origin. The rediscovery of the humanity of Jesus, and the fact of his poverty have led to a new understanding of salvation as liberation and humanization.

Salvation in its fullness belongs to the future, but its power is already present in the world. It is the power of the risen Christ, or his Spirit which is directed towards the upliftment of the oppressed out of their misery and self-hate, and the oppressor out of self-deifying tendencies. God created man and reaffirms in Jesus that people shall be fully human, not sub-human or super-human.

Someone's crying Lord

A Litany[12]

This familiar song from the Caribbean has been expanded from a South African perspective.

Someone's crying Lord, Kumba yah
   Someone's crying Lord, somewhere
   Some is millions, somewhere in many places
   There are tears of suffering
   There are tears of weakness and disappointment
   There are tears of strength and resistance
   There are tears of the rich, and tears of the poor
   Someone's crying Lord, redeem the times.

Someone's dying Lord, Kumba yah
   Some are dying of hunger and thirst
   Someone is dying because somebody else is enjoying
   Too many unnecessary and superfluous things
   Someone is dying because people go on exploiting one
      another
   Some are dying because there are structures and systems
   Which crush the poor and alienate the rich
   Someone's dying Lord
   Because we are still not prepared to take sides
   To make a choice, to be a witness
   Someone's dying Lord, redeem the times.

Someone's shouting Lord, Kumba yah
   Someone's shouting out loudly and clearly
   Someone has made a choice
   Someone is ready to stand up against the times
   Someone is shouting out

---

[12] Published in *South African Outlook*, under the title 'Litany of Human Development', December 1975, p.188.

Offering his very existence in love and anger
To fight death surrounding us
To wrestle with the evils with which we crucify each other
Someone's shouting Lord, redeem the times.

Someone's praying Lord, Kumba yah
Someone's praying Lord
We are praying in tears and anger
In frustration and weakness
In strength and endurance
We are shouting and wrestling
As Jacob wrestled with the angel
And was touched
And was marked
And became a blessing.
We are praying Lord
Spur our imagination
Sharpen our political will.
Through Jesus Christ you have let us know where you
    want us to be
Help us to be there now
Be with us, touch us, mark us, let us be a blessing
Let your power be present in our weakness
Someone's praying Lord, redeem the times.

6

The Passion
of God

The Christian life begins at the cross. In Jesus Christ crucified, God offers us God's forgiveness and saving grace. God also invites us to 'take up our cross and follow' Jesus Christ. But God does not use force like the soldiers did in making Simon of Cyrene shoulder the cross. Christian discipleship is a response of freedom and love to the suffering love of God. It is becoming caught up in the passion of God.

The place of the skull

Matthew 27:32-40, 45-46 (NIV)

As they were going out, they met a man from Cyrene, named Simon, and they forced him to carry the cross. They came to a place called Golgotha (which means the Place of the Skull). There they offered him wine to drink, mixed with gall; but after tasting it, he refused to drink it. When they had crucified him, they divided up his clothes by casting lots. And sitting down, they kept watch over him there. Above his head they placed the written charge against him: THIS IS JESUS, THE KING OF THE JEWS. Two robbers were crucified with him, one on his right and one on his left. Those who passed by hurled insults at him, shaking their heads and saying, 'You who are going to destroy the temple and build it in three days, save yourself! Come down from the cross, if you are the Son of God!'

From the sixth hour until the ninth hour darkness came over all the land. About the ninth hour Jesus cried out in a loud voice, *'Eloi, Eloi, lama sabachthani?'* — which means, 'My God, my God, why have you forsaken me?'

My God, now Jesus dies!   Axel-Ivar Berglund[13]

Throughout the centuries Christians have celebrated the drama of Good Friday and Easter through enacting the events of the passion and resurrection. In his account of a contemporary celebration of Good Friday in rural Zululand, Axel-Ivar Berglund enables us to share in the drama of the passion of God.

Maundy Thursday

It is autumn when Easter is celebrated in Zululand. The evening mists can come early, especially if the rains have been late. The smoke rises slowly towards the sky in the late afternoon of the Thursday. Wherever your eye goes it will find people on the move, all going in the same direction. All on their way to Hlobane — it is the place where Easter is to be celebrated this year.

On arrival at Hlobane you will greet everybody whom you have not seen since last year's celebration of Easter. You will greet also those whom you have seen just recently, perhaps in town or even at work. Being at Hlobane for the Easter festivities requires a greeting which brings you into a special relationship with everybody else who has arrived for the same purpose. Once having greeted you take your place in the classroom and prepare yourself for the Passover — your preparations will be quick if you are late! As soon as the sun has set the festivities will commence and nobody can afford missing any part of it.

You need not let your imagination run away with you to be able to imagine what might have taken place on the first Easter. He himself broke bread and handed the cup around personally. It takes place here at Hlobane, I am sure. As it is here, so it must have been there also.

The evening meal is soon over and the small bell strung up in a jakaranda tree calls the people together in the church. Evening has come! The moon rises slowly beyond the Hlobane mountain and casts its dim light over the compound

[13] Dr. Axel-Ivar Berglund, Lutheran pastor and authority on Zulu culture and religious symbols, wrote this unpublished account of an Easter celebration in which he participated. It has been edited for publication.

and the gathering. As the bell rings the doors that lead to the classrooms are crowded with people who are on their way to the church. They are dressed in their best — a remarkable silence has replaced the greetings and the splash of water and the crying child. Quietly they hurry along to church. You must be quiet if you are at Hlobane and it is Maundy Thursday evening and the bell has called you to the first service of the festival of Easter.

On the altar there are four candles that cast their light into the chancel of the church. In each window there is a candle. Yet, although the candles are many there is semi-light in the church. Somebody starts a hymn, everybody knows it. Immediately you are carried to the upper room on that historic Maundy Thursday when Jesus gathered his flock around him. It is a great atmosphere, filled with dignity and that majesty that you can experience only in Zululand and if it is 'iGood' — God is about to act with his people. The atmosphere grips you tight in its wonderfulness, its experience of reality, its spiritual meaningfulness. The words of the gospels overwhelm: 'And it was night!'

Good Friday

Good Friday commences early with devotions. A lay preacher reads the text of Jesus' condemnation by Pilate and with much liberty retells the story. You close your eyes and see before you Peter's denial. You hear the splash of water as Pilate washes his hands and claims to be innocent. You recall everything as if you were present.

At noon commences the three-hour service. The complete Passion is read, broken at appropriate intervals with hymns and psalms. The atmosphere is one of deep sorrow. You can feel it in the singing of the hymns, the sighs and the quietness. Nowhere is there a relaxed face and on no occasion is the singing loud and clear, free or full. When the passage of scripture has been read which relates the crucifixion the churchwarden carries the cross out through the door followed by the congregation singing again and again the hymn which they began in church. No one rushes out. No one walks straight as one otherwise would in procession —

heads are bent in sorrow. All you hear is the sound of heavy shoes and boots, heavy in reality and spirit.

The procession carries on through the gate to the road that leads up to the cemetery situated on the slopes above the church. Suddenly, as if the occasion has been that of Jerusalem long ago, a woman in the queue shouts out, 'Nkosi yami, wafa uJesu!' 'My God, now Jesus dies!'

Psalm 22:1-8

My God, my God, why have you forsaken me:
why are you so far from helping me
and from the words of my groaning?

My God, I cry to you by day, but you do not answer:
and by night also I take no rest.

But you continue holy:
you that are the praise of Israel.

In you our fathers trusted:
they trusted, and you delivered them:

To you they cried and they were saved:
they put their trust in you and were not confounded.

But as for me, I am a worm and no man:
the scorn of men and despised by the people.

All those that see me laugh me to scorn:
they shoot out their lips at me and wag their heads, saying,

'He trusted in the Lord — let him deliver him:
let him deliver him, if he delighted in him.'

Holy Saturday
The procession enters the graveyard. The churchwarden plants the cross of burden in the hole prepared. Stones are placed in the hole to keep it in place, and then earth fills the hole. The men know exactly how this is to be done, men clothed in black to mark the occasion, men who are celebrating 'iGood' at Hlobane in Zululand.

With the completion of this work everyone leaves the

graveyard. There are no words spoken and no singing. No rushing and no running. Close your eyes once more, you who are with us to see and learn, and you will experience the awesomeness of a Zulu burial. You will feel the beauty of the Zulu dignity when approaching death or when following somebody near and dear to the grave. The churchwarden who carried the cross is the last to leave. Reverently he closes the gate without looking back at the cross that now crowns the top of the hill. He closes the gate because this part of the drama has been completed. (Continued on p. 87.)

A Triumphant Shout

Pastor Z. Kameeta[14]

As the world sees it, this happening is the greatest tragedy of all time. We can discern this in the mocking, despising shouts directed at the one on the cross. Come down from the cross and save yourself! . . . He saved others, but he cannot save himself. . . . King of Israel, indeed! Let him come down from the cross, then we will believe him!

The cross of Golgotha is in the eyes of the world an indication of defeat and scandal. It is impossible for the world to believe that a Son of God the Almighty could hang from such a shameful pole. He ought to be living in a magnificent and well-defended palace. He should have a defence budget of millions of Rands, from which to purchase the most modern military weapons available and train the mightiest of armies. And his person should be guarded day and night by his soldiers. Indeed his power should be so great that, if need be, he could declare the truth a lie, and lies the truth; acts of love as acts of violence, and acts of violence as acts of love. He should have enough power to persuade God to change his mind.

In the eyes of the world, therefore, this man on the cross is a deceiver and a blasphemer, a threat to law and order. He is a weakling trying to assume the position and power of a king. But he doesn't have what it takes.

[14] Edited extracts from an unpublished sermon preached in Afrikaans by Pastor Kameeta of the Evangelical Lutheran Church at a meeting of the Namibia National Convention on Easter Sunday, 1976.

In the face of what the world requires of those who wield power, Jesus calls out from the cross in a loud voice, My God, my God, why hast thou forsaken me?

The apostles of 'law' and 'order', the protectors of Israel's identity, race and culture, hear in this cry an acknowledgement of defeat and despair. It is a confirmation of what they think of this man: a complete failure. But for those who yearn for liberation from the poisonous clutches of the evil powers it is the triumphant shout of a victorious hero!

Litany of confession

The Xhosa responses: P.T. Manci[15]

O God, in this solemn hour of remembrance we acknowledge with shame our sins that sent our Lord to the cross.

(O Lord!) We beseech you, hear us, we beseech you hear us,
O Lord, hear our prayer, we beseech you, hear us.

With penitence we confess also that we have been slow to accept the forgiveness and healing which our Lord by his death sealed as your free gift to us.

O Lord! We beseech you, hear us . . .

---

[15] The setting and translation is by Fr. Dave Dargie of Lumko Pastoral Institute.

We have not always entered into the fellowship of his sufferings, and we have charged you with indifference to our sorrow and pain.

O Lord! We beseech you, hear us . . .

All hum while one prays; then all respond
O Lord! We beseech you, hear us . . .

Singers should add in harmony parts by ear.

7

Christ is Risen —
in Zululand

The Christian life is not only being united with Christ in his death but also being raised with him in the newness of life through the power of the Spirit. The risen Christ is present in the midst of God's people wherever they gather in his name.

He is risen!

Mark 16:1-7 (NIV)

When the sabbath was over, Mary Magdalene, Mary the mother of James, and Salome bought spices so that they might go and anoint Jesus' body. Very early on the first day of the week, just after sunrise, they were on their way to the tomb and they asked each other, 'Who will roll the stone away from the entrance from the tomb?' But when they looked up, they saw that the stone, which was very large, had been rolled away. As they entered the tomb, they saw a young man dressed in a white robe sitting on the right side, and they were alarmed. 'Don't be alarmed,' he said. 'You are looking for Jesus the Nazarene. He has risen! He is not here. See the place where they laid him. But go, tell his disciples and Peter, "He is going ahead of you into Galilee. There you will see him, just as he told you."'

It is dawning!

Axel-Ivar Berglund (continued from p. 84)

The Easter Vigil

It is the night between Easter Saturday and Easter day. But although it is night and there is grass on the classroom floors of Hlobane on which to sleep, there is nobody who sleeps this night. Nobody is tired the night between Saturday and Sunday of 'iGood' — how could you be tired on this night of the greatest happening? How could you sleep when the battle between good and evil, between life and death is as intensified as it is just this night?

Two candles light up the altar. The linens have been removed. There are no flowers either for they are at the foot of the pit that held the cross on Friday. In the dark of the church one hymn after another is sung very softly and with deep reverence. The basses dominate. A woman with a fearful pitchy voice cries out in the darkness of the night but she is immediately quietened down by somebody sitting nearby. You do not shout out like that during the night between the Saturday of the rest and the Sunday of Easter. Occasionally the singing is interrupted by somebody giving some short message or making public confession of some deed done in the past, or giving a testimony of faith. But then the singing will commence, this gift of Zululand so beautiful in its many tones and modes of expression.

The closer the watch comes to dawn, the closer and more conscious becomes the atmosphere of expectation. The candles on the altar shorten. The wake proceeds. At a time suitable for the ceremony the churchwarden rises from his seat and walks to the door. He opens the door and looks out into the darkness of the night. He adjusts his coat to keep out the cold, closes the door and sits down on the mat. Nobody questions his departure. Everyone knows he is to sit there and gaze into the East to see the moment when the first signs of the new day announce its arrival.

The hinges of the door squeak as the churchwarden opens it from the outside. He puts his head into the thick air inside the church and announces with a loud and clear voice, as one moved by the occasion and with a charm which comes from a man that has followed every phase of the celebrations in the richness of the drama: *'ku Yasa!'* (It is dawning!).

As if the congregation were one they all rise in the darkness of the earliest dawn and with one voice, yet with many components, they take up the hymn known to all which has been set aside for the occasion. They sing as if there has been no tiredness and wake. They sing as if there had been a change in life. They sing as those liberated from their throats and with the width of their mouths:

> At dawn, at the rising of the sun
> Mary Magdalene went out
> with sweetsmelling balms to the grave
> in order to smear Jesus there.
> Halleluja! Halleluja!

In procession the congregation moves from the closed atmosphere of the church to the chill of the morning air of the graveyard. The steps are quick and light, and the melody of the hymn is quick and brisk inviting you to join in had you not done so before. Led by the officiating minister in alb and white stole, the congregation passes through the gates to the road that leads to the cemetery. A jubilant multitude singing at the top of their voices and with such excitement that could carry the whole world. The hymn has been repeated three times by now, and the fourth time is commenced as the last members pass through the gate and take their places around the black cross of Friday. A glance at the sky tells you that within minutes the sun will rise and fill the whole of the shivering community with the warmth of its rays.

Easter Day
The service at the graveyard is just about to begin when the minister is interrupted by a woman who shouts out, *'iNkosi ivukile!'* (The Lord is risen!) You recognise her voice as that of the woman who cried out in her despair on Friday. Although her voice is neither very beautiful or otherwise significant, the words are filled with meaning for the people gathered at the cemetery this Easter day at Hlobane in Zululand.

By the time the jubilant service has come to a close the sun has long warmed the cold of the morning. The service over, everybody goes down to the church for breakfast. There is no procession now, and the laughter and joy, the talk and singing which takes place amongst the graves at Hlobane cemetery on Sunday morning of 'iGood' comes naturally, replacing the restraint and great quiet of the past two days.

At nine o'clock the concluding service begins. It is Easter day and the singing is great and the choirs many. The altar is clothed again. The sermon is short but jubilant and there is the eucharist with him who today is risen from the dead. This is not the last supper, but the feast of joy and thankfulness. You breathe it in the atmosphere. You breathe it in the faces of the people. You breathe it in the service. There is life, life which has risen from the dead. Today he is risen! He has returned to the living again. His power is today mightier than ever before because today he has broken down death and given us health and life again.

A Confession of Faith   Klaus Nürnberger[16]

Taken from a Proposed Confession of Faith for the Church in Southern Africa written by Dr Nürnberger, Professor Theology at the University of South Africa.

I believe in Jesus Christ,
who came, in the authority of God, to share our misery,
who voluntarily became the victim of our enmity against our
    Creator
to redeem us from sin, evil, and death,
from oppression and exploitation,
from greed and craving for power,
from hatred and suspicion,
from self-aggrandisement and arbitrariness,
from our fear of each other and of the future,
from our enslavement by drugs and sorcery,
by prejudice and traditions that separate us,
by ideologies of race, class, ethnicity or family,
by detrimental programmes and static structures.

Who rose from the dead
to endow us all with his new life,
a life in freedom and joy,
a life in brotherly love,

---

[16] Published in the *Journal of Theology for Southern Africa*, no. 32, September 1980, p.60.

a life in common service to the benefit of all,
a life struggling against poverty and injustice,
against sickness and ignorance,
a life in responsibility for those that will
come after us and inhabit our land,
a life which witnesses to his salvation in word and deed,
a life assured of his rule,
a life of hope in his future for us all.

Acclamation

Arranged in Zulu: L. Mpotulo

Alleluia — alleluia, alleluia! *(twice)*
Christ has died — Christ has died, Christ is risen *(twice)*
Christ will come — Christ will come again, alleluia! *(twice)*

Encountered by Jesus

The Christian life is awakened within us when we are encountered by the grace of God in Jesus Christ. It is he who finds us, not we who find him; his grace reaches out to us enabling us to respond in faith and love.

Lost and found

Luke 15:1-7 (JB)

The tax collector and the sinners, meanwhile, were all seeking his company to hear what he had to say, and the Pharisees and the scribes complained. 'This man' they said, 'welcomes sinners and eats with them.' So he spoke this parable to them:

'What man among you with a hundred sheep, losing one, would not leave the ninety-nine in the wilderness and go after the missing one till he found it? And when he found it, would he not joyfully take it upon his shoulders and then, when he got home, call together his friends and neighbours? "Rejoice with me," he would say, "I have found my sheep that was lost." In the same way, I tell you, there will be more rejoicing in heaven over one repentant sinner than over ninety-nine virtuous men who have no need of repentance.'

Raised to new life

Romans 5:20-21, 6:1-4 (NIV)

Where sin increased, grace increased all the more, so that, just as sin reigned in death, so also grace might reign through righteousness to bring eternal life through Jesus Christ our Lord. What shall we say, then? Shall we go on sinning, so that grace may increase? By no means! We died to sin; how can we live in it any longer? Or don't you know that all of us who were baptised into Christ Jesus were baptised into his death? We were therefore buried with him through baptism into death in order that, just as Christ was raised from the dead through the glory of the Father, we too may live a new life.

What Jesus means to me
Desmond Tutu[17]

The worst sin in our society is to have failed. We work ourselves into a frazzle in order to succeed, in order to be accepted, and we cannot understand that we should certainly not carry this attitude over into our relationship with God.

What a tremendous relief it is to discover that we don't need to prove ourselves to God. We don't have to do anything at all to be acceptable to him. That is what Jesus came to say, 'Hey, you don't have to earn God's love. It is not a matter of human achievement. Man you are, you exist, because God loves you already. You are a child of divine love.' The Pharisees, the religious leaders of his day — the bishops and presidents and moderators — they couldn't buy that! Jesus tried to tell them all sorts of stories to prove this point, like the one about the labourers in the vineyard who were hired in batches at different times of the day. With all but the very last lot the owner of the vineyard came to an agreement about the wages. The last lot worked for no time at all and yet they were paid a full day's wage — God's love and compassion are given freely and without measure. They are not earned. They are totally unmerited and gracious.

Jesus really scandalised the religious leaders. He ate with the riffraff and the scum — those were the ones with whom

[17] Bishop Desmond Tutu is Anglican Bishop of Johannesburg and Nobel Peace Prize Winner for 1984. This is an edited extract from an address entitled 'What Jesus means to me', given at the University of Natal in August 1981, and published in *Hope and Suffering*, Eerdmans, Grand Rapids, and Skotaville, Johannesburg, 1983, pp.89ff.

he hobnobbed because he had come to seek and find the lost. And as a physician he was needed by those who were sick, not the whole (or those who thought they were whole and righteous).

The good news is that God loves me long before I can do anything to deserve it. He is like the father of the prodigal son, waiting anxiously for the return of his wayward son and when he sees this feckless creature appearing on the horizon, rushes out to meet, embrace and kiss him — no recriminations, asking only that the fatted calf be slaughtered, a ring be placed on his finger and the best robe put on him; and they must rejoice in a party to celebrate because his lost one has been found, this dead one has been brought to life again. God is like the Good Shepherd who goes looking for the lost sheep, the troublesome, obstreperous sheep with its wool torn and probably stuck in a ditch of dirty water. When he finds it he carries it on his shoulder and calls his friends to celebrate with him.

That is tremendous stuff — that is the good news. 'Whilst we were yet sinners' says St Paul, 'Christ died for us.' God did not wait until we were die-able, for he could then have waited until the cows come home. No, whilst we were God's enemies he accepted us. God loves us, says Jesus, not because we are lovable, but we are lovable because God loves us. That has liberated me, it has given me the assurance of being a child in his father's home. I am loved. That is the most important fact about me and nothing, absolutely nothing can change that fact. All I do now is an expression of my gratitude for what God has already done for me in Christ Jesus my Lord and Saviour.

Further, Jesus attests my infinite value as a child of God. While he is rushing to the house of Jairus to be with Jairus' dying daughter, Jesus stops to attend to the woman with a haemorrhage; or he will speak directly to one person in a crowd, like Zacchaeus. You know something, we are each a temple, a tabernacle, a sanctuary of the Holy Spirit, of Jesus, of God. Yes, God dwells in you, you are a God-carrier. That is why it is blasphemy for God's children to be treated as if they were things, uprooted from their homes and dumped in

Encountered by Jesus

arid resettlement camps. Jesus says to do that to those he called the least of his brethren is to do it to him.

This Jesus affirms me and says that I matter, and so I can have a proper self-assurance. Just note how Jesus was able to get a prostitute like Mary Magdalene to become a saint. He mentioned the quality in her which nobody else had noticed — her great capacity to love, and from selling her body she became one of his most loyal followers.

Anthony Bloom, the Orthodox master of the spiritual life, tells the story of a simple Russian country priest who was confronted by an eminent scientist. The scientist trotted out apparently devastating arguments against the existence of God and declared, 'I don't believe in God'. The unlettered priest retorted quickly, 'Oh, it doesn't matter — God believes in you.' That is what Jesus says to me — God believes in you. Can you believe that — you and I, who have been buried with Christ in baptism and raised to a new life of righteousness with him, are, despite all appearances to the contrary, princes and princesses together with Christ.

The Hound of Heaven   Alan Paton[18]

The following extract and poem are part of Alan Paton's reflections on the life of St Francis of Assisi which he published in Instrument of Thy Peace. *The reading and the poem are separated in that book by* 'The Hound of Heaven' *by Francis Thompson which describes God's persistence in searching for us. This I believe provides the key to understanding Paton's poem.*

Why did Jesus hold spellbound those who listened to him? It was because he showed them that they were not helpless victims in the grip of fears, hates, the past, the world. They were the salt of the earth, the light of the world. He showed them a new thing — that freedom and obedience are insepar- able. For where is the joy of living in a society in which all

---

[18] Alan Paton, *An Instrument of Thy Peace*, Seabury, New York, 1968, p.121f. The poem, written in 1946-7 shortly before Paton wrote *Cry the Beloved Country*, was originally entitled 'The Prison House' and is full of images derived from his experience as princi- pal of a boys' reformatory.

obey and none is free? Or in which all are free and none obeys? Something in them rose up to meet him; they were caught up into the bondage which is the perfect freedom; they became his servants and his freedmen; they became his followers and his disciples; in him they found meaning for their lives, and there is no freedom like the freedom of finding meaning for one's life, of becoming the instrument of a Lord who helps us to be what we were meant to be. Yet many resist him, believing that to follow him is to lose the whole world.

He met me at the door

I ran from the prison house but they captured me,
And he waited at the door with a face of doom,
And he motioned me to go to his private room,
And he took my rank from me and gave me the hell
Of his tongue, and he ordered me to the runaway cell
With the walls and the chains and the long night-days and
    the gloom.

And once on leave that goes to the well-behaved
I rose in fright from the very brothel bed
And through the midnight streets like a mad thing fled
Sobbing with fear lest the door be closed on me,
But nothing he did to me, he let me be,
No word but your clothing's disarranged he said.

And once in a place where I was, a man did ask
Whence I was, and he said, I never thought to see
A man from that place, and I wish I could be
In that place, by God I wish that I could be there,
I wish I was there, and I went back on air
And he met me there at the door, and he smiled at me.

And once when he took the whip to my rebel flesh
With foul and magnificent words I cursed and reviled
His name and his house and his works, and drunken and wild
I took the whip from his hands and slashed him again
And again and again, so he paid the price for my pain,
Till I fell at his feet and wept on a stone like a child.

He can take the hide from my back, and the sight from my
  eyes,
The lust of my loins, and the comforts of my memory,
Fruit's taste, and the scent of the flowers, the salt of the sea,
The sounds of the world, and the words of magic and fire
That comforted me, so long as he does not require
The chains that now are become like garments to me.

Powerful is the Gospel

Lead   Hlanganani ma Krestu
Response Hlanganani *(Four times)*
iKhona lehlanganu ya ma Krestu *(Four times)*

Lead   Powerful is the Gospel
Response Very powerful *(Four times)*
I have already told you it is very powerful *(Four times)*

Wonderful is the Gospel . . . (etc)

Conversion to Christ

The Christian life involves a radical change in our lives. Such a transformation may begin with unexpected suddenness. Or it may begin imperceptibly so that our awareness of what God is doing in us only gradually comes to consciousness. But the Christian life always has a moment of beginning however difficult it might be to give that moment a precise date or hour. And it is always a process, no matter how dramatic its beginning, a process of personal healing and social consequences.

The conversion of Paul   Acts 9:1-19 (RSV)

But Saul, still breathing threats and murder against the disciples of the Lord, went to the high priest and asked him for letters to the synagogues at Damascus, so that if he found any belonging to the Way, men or women, he might bring them bound to Jerusalem. Now as he journeyed he approached Damascus, and suddenly a light from heaven flashed about him. And he fell to the ground and heard a voice saying to him, 'Saul, Saul, why do you persecute me?' And he said, 'Who are you, Lord?' And he said, 'I am Jesus, whom you are persecuting; but rise and enter the city, and you will be told what you are to do.' The men who were travelling with him stood speechless, hearing the voice but seeing no one. Saul arose from the ground; and when his eyes were opened, he could see nothing; so they led him by the hand and brought him into Damascus. And for three days he was without sight, and neither ate nor drank.

Now there was a disciple at Damascus named Ananias. The Lord said to him in a vision, 'Ananias.' And he said, 'Here I am, Lord.' And the Lord said to him, 'Rise and go to the street named Straight, and inquire in the house of Judas for a man of Tarsus named Saul; for behold, he is praying, and he has seen a man named Ananias come in and lay his hands on him so that he might regain his sight.' But Ananias answered, 'Lord, I have heard from many about this man, how much evil he has done to thy saints at Jerusalem; and here he has authority from the chief priests to bind all who call upon thy name.' But the Lord said to him, 'Go, for he is a chosen instrument of mine to carry my name to the Gentiles and kings and the sons of Israel; for I will show him how much he must suffer for the sake of my name.' So Ananias departed and entered the house. And laying his hands on him he said, 'Brother Saul, the Lord Jesus who appeared to you on the road by which you came, has sent me that you may regain your sight and be filled with the Holy Spirit.' And immediately something like scales fell from his eyes and he regained his sight. Then he rose and was baptised, and took food and was strengthened.

The love of Christ impelled me   David Livingstone[19]

Although the nineteenth century European missionaries often became instruments of colonialism, whether by choice or inadvertently, the original impulse for their work derived from their conversion to Christ. This enabled them to endure enormous hardships for the sake of the gospel. David Livingstone arrived in South Africa in 1841. This extract from his Missionary Travels and Researches in South Africa, *shows how the love of Christ led him to devote his life to the alleviation of human misery, and the struggle against the slave trade.*

Great pains had been taken by my parents to instil the doctrines of Christianity into my mind, and I had no difficulty in understanding the theory of free salvation by the atonement of our Saviour, but it was only about this time that I began to

---

[19] David Livingstone, *Missionary Travels and Researches in South Africa,* John Murray, London, 1912, p.4. First published in 1857.

feel the necessity of a personal application of the doctrine to my own case. The change was like what may be supposed would take place where it is possible to cure a case of 'colour blindness'. The fullness with which the pardon of all our guilt is offered in God's book drew forth feelings of affectionate love to him who bought us with his blood, which in some small measure has influenced my conduct ever since. But I shall not again refer to the inner spiritual life which I believe then began, nor do I intend to specify with any prominence the evangelistic labours to which the love of Christ impelled me: this book will speak not so much of what has been done, as to what still remains to be performed before the gospel can be said to be preached to all nations. In the glow of love which Christianity inspires, I soon resolved to devote my life to the alleviation of human misery.

I let myself go

Edgar Brookes[20]

In his autobiography, A South African Pilgrimage, *Edgar Brookes describes his long political and spiritual journey during which he became an outspoken critic of racial injustice as well as a deeply committed Christian. In 1937 Dr. Brookes became a Senator representing blacks, but this ended with the advent of apartheid. On his retirement as Professor of History at the University of Natal, Dr. Brookes was ordained an Anglican priest.*

The subject of the Dark Ages, the decline and fall of the Christian Roman Empire of the West and its somewhat spectral resurrection as the Holy Roman Empire had interested me as early as my seventeenth year, and has remained a vivid interest ever since. As I surveyed my changing world, the visible decline of Great Britain and the extraordinary revolutions of the Commonwealth, I thought much of the Roman Empire in the fifth century. As the skies darkened more and more over my own South Africa, my mind went naturally to the experience and the philosophy of St Augustine, the great North African. Like him I was led to the ultimate loyalty, the City of God, which transcends all human

[20] Edgar Brookes, *A South African Pilgrimage,* Ravan, Johannesburg 1977, p.117f.

patriotisms. Like him I realised that the City of God, although most nearly institutionalised in the Church, contained many people who were outside the Church and could not contain some who were inside it. Like him I came to believe that the City of God was made up of all those who loved God to the contempt of self, and the earthly city — the *civitas terrena* — of all those who loved self to the contempt of God. Like him I believed, and began dimly to see, that God was still in charge in the midst of our human tragedies, that there is

> one far-off divine event
> To which the whole creation moves

and though it may be far-off it is still divine. All these thoughts I tried to put into my book (*The City of God and the Politics of Crisis*[21]), and writing it, though much in it was sorrowful, was a real joy.

I feel that it was during the time that I was meditating on this great work of St Augustine that my Christian faith became more deeply rooted and mature. I remember thinking as I walked across the University playing-fields that there is a doubt which is not really intellectual, but an infirmity of the will of which the powers of evil make use, that one might well reverse Tennyson's lines to read

> There lives more faith in all the Creeds,
> Believe me, than in honest doubt.

I know that I had honestly striven to test my faith intellectually, that there was no lack of intellectual integrity in my faith, that the miracles of unbelief were to me far greater stumbling-blocks than the miracles of belief. I felt that I need not be apologetic to myself or anyone else for accepting the faith which was good enough for the minds of John Henry Newman, Gilbert Keith Chesterton and William Temple. I knew too that my affection and desire went out to my Lord, and yet there was an infirmity of will that prevented me from really giving of my utmost. I doubted though I did not really

[21] Edgar H. Brookes, *The City of God and the Politics of Crisis*, Oxford University Press, 1960.

doubt. Then I asked myself, 'How long is this to go on? How long before, in honest intellectual integrity and adoring love, I let myself go?' Was I to wait until I was sixty? Or seventy? Or eighty? Surely the truest and loveliest thing to do was to let go now and throw myself completely upon God, and live as one who truly believes. And so I did, and the riches of power, peace, love and strength which this has given me are not easily to be set down in words.

Healing means personal and social conversion
Bonganjalo Goba[22]

The conversion experience is a personal transformation that involves a change from an old primary allegiance to a new commitment to God in Christ. It is a change which brings about healing and liberation because it involves the freeing of soul, body and mind from the oppressive structures of guilt and alienation. White and black Christians need to be set free from the false political consciousness which results from participation or acquiescence in oppressive structures. Such liberation requires *metanoia*, or repentance, for such radical change is the prerequisite of God's healing grace. Healing thus means undergoing deep spiritual and social conversion.

The black Christian community in South Africa is challenged to provide a context in which such personal transformation can take place. It is called to be a healing, liberating community that encourages and enables God's liberating work of deep spiritual as well as social conversion. A community that fosters a counter-ethos whose orientation is imbued with the liberating spirit of God revealed in Jesus Christ. Thus it is called to provide a context in which both blacks and whites are challenged to re-examine their allegiance, in terms of the existing socio-political structures, and commit their lives to the liberating power of the Holy Spirit. This will challenge all oppressive structures in our society.

[22] An edited extract from Bonganjalo Goba, 'The Role of the Black Church in the Process of Healing Human Brokenness,' *Journal of Theology for South Africa*, no. 28, September 1979, p.11f. Dr. Goba is a minister of the United Congregational Church, and a theologian teaching at the University of South Africa.

Renew a right spirit within me

Psalm 51:1-12, 17

Have mercy on me, O God, in your enduring goodness:
according to the fullness of your compassion
    blot out my offences.

Wash me thoroughly from my wickedness:
and cleanse me from my sin.

For I acknowledge my rebellion:
and my sin is ever before me.

Against you only have I sinned
    and done what is evil in your eyes:
so you will be just in your sentence
    and blameless in your judging.

Surely in wickedness I was brought to birth:
and in sin my mother conceived me.

You that desire truth in the inward parts:
O teach me wisdom in the secret places of the heart.

Purge me with hyssop, and I shall be clean:
wash me, and I shall be whiter than snow.

Make me hear of joy and gladness:
let the bones which you have broken rejoice.

Hide your face from my sins:
and blot out all my iniquities.

Create in me a clean heart, O God:
and renew a right spirit within me.

Do not cast me out from your presence:
do not take your holy spirit from me.

O give me the gladness of your help again:
and support me with a willing spirit.

The sacrifice of God is a broken spirit:
a broken and contrite heart, O God, you will not despise.

10

Christ on Robben Island

The Christian life may begin in what appear to be the most unlikely places. Jesus Christ comes to us where we are, and where we may least expect to meet him. He certainly visits prisons as much as he does sanctuaries. When he comes it is often with an invitation to a particular task.

Prisoner for Christ

Philippians 1:12-26 (JB)

I am glad to tell you, brothers, that the things which happened to me have actually been a help to the Good News. My chains, in Christ, have become famous not only all over the Praetorium but everywhere, and most of the brothers have taken courage in the Lord from these chains of mine and are getting more and more daring in announcing the Message without any fear. It is true that some of them are doing it just out of rivalry and competition, but the rest preach Christ with the right intention, out of nothing but love, as they know that this is my invariable way of defending the gospel. The others, who proclaim Christ for jealous or selfish motives, do not mind if they make my chains heavier to bear. But does it matter? Whether from dishonest motives or in sincerity, Christ is proclaimed; and that makes me happy; and I shall continue to be happy, because I know this will help to save me, thanks to your prayers and to the help which will be given me by the Spirit of Jesus. My one hope and trust is that I shall never have to admit defeat, but that now as always I shall have the courage for Christ to be glorified in my body, whether by my life or by my death. Life for me, of course, is Christ. . . .

He visited me in prison
Stanley Mogoba

Stanley Mogoba, now the General Secretary of the Methodist Church of South Africa, was detained in prison on Robben Island, off the coast of Cape Town, between 1963-6. Mr Mogoba was arrested because he was suspected of encouraging young people to engage in revolutionary activity. In his own words: 'I had been a member of the African National Congress Youth League when it was still legal. At that time I was involved with the Pan-African Congress, but I was not a card carrying member. In fact I was just a passive adherent to whom young people came for advice. The major evidence against me at my trial was that I had advised the burning of a Dutch Reformed Church. Ironically, I had strongly advised the young people against this. So I went to gaol for having saved a Dutch Reformed church!' The following is an edited account of the Revd. Stanley Mogoba's experience as told to the author.

I well remember the Sunday before my arrest. It was Passion Sunday, and I, a Methodist local preacher, was preaching in Atteridgeville near Pretoria on the theme 'The Suffering Servant'. A week later I was arrested. How ironical it was that I myself was now behind bars.

I was eight months in prison, part of the time in isolation, awaiting trial. During that time I prayed and read the Bible a great deal. In fact, during isolation I read the Bible from cover to cover for it was the only literature I had. I also remember conducting services on Sundays, and longing for Holy Communion. But there was no bread and wine, and no minister to celebrate the sacrament. I remember Christmas 1963 in particular. This was my first Christmas out of normal society. We held a service that day. We were also served rotten mealies!

After being sentenced, conditions changed slightly for the better, except for the gruesome journey in a police van from Johannesburg to Cape Town. Then we arrived on Robben Island, a gaol like any other only a little more strict I discovered. I well remember going through many difficult times, including a hundred hour hunger strike. As a result of this I was placed in solitary confinement without even a Bible.

Before this time of isolation I had been working with a group of nearly two hundred inmates. We were a community and although the conditions were difficult we were together and it was good. When I entered the isolation cell I remember saying, 'well, now I am going to have a little bit of a retreat'. I did not know it was to be six months long. Having nothing to read was a special trial. It was during this time that I composed a poem entitled 'Cement'.

An unprecedented abundance of cement
Below, above and all around
A notorious capacity to retain cold
Without an equal facility for warmth

Inside is captured a column of air
And a solid mass of human substance
A pertinent question poses itself:
Which loses heat to which?

As complete an enclosure as possible
Throwing its presence all around
Until recognised by all five senses
Achieving the results of refrigeration.

Hovering relentlessly is the stubborn stillness
Permeating both solid and gas
A free play of winged imagination
And the inevitable introspection
Stretch themselves painfully over
The reluctant minutes of the marathon day.[23]

At this time I met Denis Brutus who played a very important part in my Christian pilgrimage. He was doing a short

[23] First published in the anthology, Robert Royston (ed.), *To Whom it May Concern*, A.D. Donker, Cape Town, 1973. Now also published in Tim Couzens and Essop Patel (eds.), *The Return of the Aamasi Bird: Black South African Poetry, 1891-1981*, Ravan, Johannesburg, 1982, p.220.

eighteen months sentence and while cleaning the passage outside my cell, when no one was listening, he used to talk to me. It was he who brought me a book called *The Human Christ* by a Roman Catholic whose name I cannot recall. I hid it in my blankets and when nobody was about I read it, particularly at night. It brought me to my call to the ministry.

I was reading the portion of the book which describes the story of the rich young man who came to Jesus. I had read it often and even preached on it. But for some reason it now caused turmoil in my spirit, a turmoil which I could not understand because I, clad in prison khaki clothes, was anything but a rich man! I tried to put the book aside, but I could not sleep. I was deeply disturbed. Then I realised that Christ was trying to say something to me even though my circumstances were so different to that of the rich man. What touched me so deeply was that the writer of *The Human Christ* focused on Christ, the Christ who was so sad to see the young man go, the sorrow of Christ when he saw him unable to take the final step to true fulfilment. So both the young man and Christ were sad, and now a third party was unhappy too.

I remained unhappy for some time pondering what all this meant. Perhaps I was being called to serve Christ in a new way once I had left the Island. But it was only when I said 'I will follow you now, I am prepared to give my entire life to you and enter the ministry' that my sorrow left me and I experienced a sense of joy which I had never had before and which still sustains me when I feel weak.

Of course, I had been approached before about becoming a minister but I had laughed it off. I was a teacher when arrested and was planning to study Law. In fact I had already registered through the University of South Africa to study Law and my books had just arrived before I went into isolation. But now, as I felt called to abandon the study of Law for the Christian ministry, I also felt the emptiness of justice having myself become a subject of injustice.

It was, nevertheless, not an easy decision to make in that environment, especially as I had to face my fellow prisoners and tell them. Some thought I had gone mad, others that I had been softened up. But I assured them that my political convictions had not changed, that I was with them, but now much more as a committed Christian with a vocation. Still, many could not understand how someone who had gone through all this suffering would want to embark on such a ' career.

This was a critical point of testing. I had now to relate my new direction in life to my political ideas and commitments, and, moreover, to my political companions. In doing so I had difficulty in getting a minister with whom I could discuss my situation, and I did not have a Bible. I was being called into the ministry without a Bible! Only later was I given a Xhosa Bible, even though I did not know any Xhosa. But that is how I learnt to read and understand it. Beginning with the Gospels I finally read the whole Bible in Xhosa.

Our case, resulting from the hunger strike, was not over. Eventually we were punished severely with cuts. One of my fellow prisoners said: 'No, I really don't want to have anything to do with this Christ you tell about'. But for me Christ was a very real help at this time for he had come to me in my suffering.

Imprisoned by riches   Luke 18:18-25 (NIV)

A certain ruler asked him, 'Good teacher, what must I do to inherit eternal life?' 'Why do you call me good?' Jesus answered. 'No one is good — except God alone. You know the commandments: "Do not commit adultery, do not murder, do not steal, do not give false testimony, honour your father and mother."' 'All of these I have kept since I was a boy,' he said. When Jesus heard this, he said to him, 'You still lack one thing. Sell everything you have and give to the poor, and you will have treasure in heaven. Then come, follow me.' When he heard this, he became very sad, because he was a man of great wealth. Jesus looked at him and said, 'How hard it is for the rich to enter the kingdom of God! Indeed, it is easier for a camel to go through the eye of a needle than for a rich man to enter the kingdom of God.'

No matter if I am in prison — God is love

A Xhosa hymn: J. Nduna

God is love . . . God is love . . . God is love . . . Alleluia!
God is love . . . God is love . . . God is love . . . Alleluia!

No matter if I am lonely — Ahe! — God is love, alleluia.
No matter if I am hungry — Ahe! — God is love, alleluia.
God is love . . .

No matter if I'm in prison Ahe! — God is love, alleluia.
No matter if I am tortured — Ahe! — God is love, alleluia.
God is love . . .

No matter if they oppress me — Ahe! — God is love, alleluia.
No matter if he delays long — Ahe! — God is love, alleluia.
God is love . . .

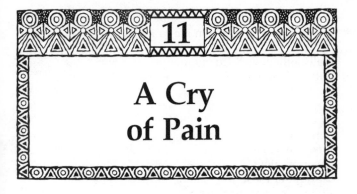

11

A Cry
of Pain

The Christian life includes a growing sensitivity to the pain and suffering of other people.

My heart fails me

Jeremiah 8:18-23 (JB)

Sorrow overtakes me,
my heart fails me.
Listen, the cry of the daughter of my people
sounds throughout the land,
'Yahweh no longer in Zion?
Her King no longer in her?'
(Why have they provoked me with their carved images,
with these Nothings from foreign countries?)
'The harvest is over, summer at an end,
and we have not been saved!'
The wound of the daughter of my people wounds me too,
all looks dark to me, terror grips me.
Is there not balm in Gilead any more?
Is there no doctor there?
Then why does it make no progress,
this cure of the daughter of my people?
Who will turn my head into a fountain,
and my eyes into a spring of tears,
so that I may weep all day, all night,
for all the dead out of the daughter of my people?

My heart cries out

Helen Kotze[24]

My heart cries out within me as I watch
Affluent whites go by
Well clothed, well fed, secure
Within their circle,
Privilege.
How many care, or even think
Of those
Deprived by their very having?
I see one smile
Superior, aloof,
Scornful of those who stand,
And seeing not their placards,
Caring not for truth
Thus starkly told.

The others walking by —
Non-citizens, non people,
Called Non-whites —
They understand too well.
Theirs is a daily knowledge,
Part of life,
A constant pain and anguish
Like a knife
Which turns within their hearts.

My heart cries out within me,
But my eyes are dry,
And hollow is my hope.

A Cry for Justice

Denis Hurley[25]

*From a sermon preached by the Catholic Archbishop of Durban,
Denis Hurley OMI, in Pietermaritzburg in August 1972 after student
unrest in response to Black student protest against educational
injustices.*

[24] Originally entitled 'Reflections at a Black Sash Stand' this poem was published in
Pro Veritate, September 1974. The Black Sash is an organisation of white women who
have protested against apartheid during the past three decades. *Pro Veritate* was an
independant ecumenical monthly journal originally edited by Dr. Beyers Naude.
[25] Published in *Pro Veritate,* 15 September 1972.

Christ, with whom we associate ourselves in this celebration of the Eucharist, is a person not unacquainted with pain. In becoming man, in assuming our human nature, he took on the possibility and the reality of pain — to the point where on the cross the terrible plaint was wrung from him: 'My God, my God, why have you abandoned me?'

There is Christian courage, Christian fortitude, in the bearing of pain. But the silent toleration of pain is not an absolute — not a supreme value. Christianity is not stoicism. There are times when it is not only permissible but obligatory to reveal our pain. For pain is the sign of something that is wrong, a diminution of life, a threat to life. To reveal pain is to reveal the truth and revelation of the truth is frequently a sacred duty.

So it is that during the past few weeks the truth has been revealed to us in a most vivid way through the cry of pain of black university students. This particular revelation began with the speech of Mr Abram Tiro on Graduation Day at the University of the North. Mr Tiro was expelled for making that speech. The truth he was revealing is a long-standing one — the truth of the humiliation experienced by black students, only a small segment — but a very important segment — of the humiliation experienced by all the black peoples of South Africa. It is not a cry for pity, but a cry for redress, a cry for justice, a cry revealing that people cannot live for ever under a system which denies them the full expression of their humanity.

The cry of pain that went up from Turfloop and was echoed around the country, a cry of pain revealing explicitly the suffering of black students under the restrictions and humiliations they experience, but implicitly calling attention to all that is involved in the experience of being black in South Africa: poverty, starvation, ill-health, the high incidence of family disruption, promiscuity, infidelity, insecurity and violence; a genocidal child mortality; restrictions on education, on employment, on movement, on housing; the almost total privation of political rights. The cry of pain elicited by all this has been heard often and from many quarters, and the awful dishonour of white South Africa is

113

the dismal facility with which it has turned a deaf ear.

The white students have not closed their ears. This time again they have heard the cry of pain and have responded with Christian solicitude — to the point of suffering violence for their concern. The important thing is now that all to whom the cry of pain of the black students means anything must dedicate themselves to ensuring that this cry is clearly and unmistakably interpreted to white South Africa.

Events such as the ones we are experiencing at present shake us out of our complacency. The cracking of complacency is a wonderful thing, but it is only the beginning of the task. An immense effort lies ahead of us — the effort of church people to dissolve the hard crust of habit and custom inconsistent with the gospel and allow the true face of Christian concern, recognition and sharing to break through and be a witness to our faith; the effort of students to maintain their concern for truth and justice, not only at university but afterwards in the far more difficult circumstances of career and family building; the effort to interpret our faith, our concern, our understanding of the cry of pain of the oppressed people to those with power.

If it is hard for us who are gathered here to break the hard crust of habit and custom, it is a thousand times harder for those with power. All sorts of blindnesses, prejudices and mistaken traditions must go by the board so that the cry of pain may be heard for what it truly is and there may be a genuine human and Christian response.

It looks so hopeless, so desperately hopeless. So much has been tried already and so much has failed. We are up against some of the most powerful and tenacious instincts of humanity: the herd instinct, the power instinct, the possessive instinct — in others, and, if we really look in our hearts, in ourselves as well; instincts that are so much part of us that we scarcely notice how inconsistent their manifestations are with the Christian ideals that we proclaim. It is in this context that Jesus uttered the words: 'Truly, truly, I say to you, unless a grain of wheat falls into the earth and dies, it remains alone; but if it die, it bears much fruit. He who loves his life, loses it, and he who hates his life in this world, will

A cry of pain

keep it for eternal life'.

Jesus spoke often of death and suffering. He realised that his was a mission of suffering and death. But he knew too, that it did not stop there, that there was something beyond death — resurrection and new life. As we rededicate ourselves to a mission of truth and justice we know that it will not be realised without experiences of suffering and death; but the undying hope that is part of every human heart, the undying hope that has been sharpened and illuminated and consecrated by Christ, tells us that beyond that experience lies the possibility that South Africa will rise above all it has been to become part of the human family in which humanity means more than colour, justice more than power, dignity and freedom more than ease and opulence. It is a desperate hope, but it is still a hope, and to this hope we dedicate ourselves.

My eyes overflow with tears   Jeremiah 14:17-22 (NIV)

Speak this word to them:

> 'Let my eyes overflow with tears
> night and day without ceasing;
> for my virgin daughter — my people —
>   has suffered a grievous wound,
>   a crushing blow.
> If I go into the country,
>   I see those slain by the sword;
> If I go into the city,
>   I see the ravages of famine.
> Both prophet and priest
>   have gone to a land they know not.'
> Have you rejected Judah completely?
>   Do you despise Zion?
> Why have you afflicted us
>   so that we cannot be healed?
> We hoped for peace
>   but no good has come,
> for a time of healing

but there is only terror.
O Lord, we acknowledge our wickedness
    and the guilt of our fathers;
    we have indeed sinned against you.
For the sake of your name do not despise us;
    do not dishonour your glorious throne.
Remember your covenant with us
    and do not break it.
Do any of the worthless idols of the nations bring rain?
    Do the skies themselves send down showers?
No, it is you, O Lord our God.
    Therefore our hope is in you,
    for you are the one who does all this.

Answer me, O Lord

A Sotho Prayer: T.W. Suping

Answer me, O Lord, Answer me, O Lord
    Lord how great is your mercy.

Answer me, O Lord, Answer me, O Lord,
    Save your people in your love.

The Absence of God

The Christian life is no stranger to doubt and despair. There come times when events around us or personal experiences make it very difficult to believe and therefore to pray. It is as though God is absent. Life no longer has any meaning or purpose.

Curse the day Job 3:1-10 (JB)

In the end it was Job who broke the silence and cursed the day of his birth. This is what he said:

May the day perish when I was born,
    and the night that told of a boy conceived.
May that day be darkness,
    may God on high have no thought for it,
    may no light shine on it.
May murk and deep shadow claim it for their own,
    clouds hang over it,
    eclipse swoop down on it.
Yes, let the dark lay hold of it,
    to the days of the year let it be not joined,
    into the reckoning of months not find its way.
May that night be dismal,
    no shout of joy come near it.
Let them curse it who curse the day,
    who are prepared to rouse Leviathan.
Dark be the stars of its morning,

let it wait in vain for light
and never see the opening eyes of dawn.
Since it would not shut the doors of the womb on me
to hide sorrow from my eyes.

The Lord has gone

Maria Zotwana[26]

Forced removals of black people in South Africa have been one of the most destructive aspects of the policy of apartheid. Whole communities of people have been uprooted from the land and homes where they have lived, often for generations, and dumped elsewhere in order to rationalise 'separate development'. Immense suffering, bitterness and a sense of hopelessness has resulted. At the end of 1977 four hundred Mfengu families were removed from their Tsitsikama home after living there since 1835 on land granted them by the Cape Colonial administration. They were dumped in the Ciskei at Elukhanyweni with less land, fewer jobs, lower wages and poorer diets. An old person, Maria Zotwana, described her situation:

We had no choice; the guns were behind us, then they bring us to this sad place. Here there is not enough food. I am hungry now, as I am sitting here. Everybody has died. My man has gone and died, as have my daughters. They took my land away. The Lord has also gone, yes, I suppose he has also gone.

God has forgotten

Psalm 10:1-5, 10-12

Why do you stand far off, O Lord:
why do you hide your face in time of need?

The ungodly in their pride persecute the poor:
let them be caught in the schemes they have devised.

For the ungodly man boasts of his heart's desire:
he grasps at profit, he spurns and blasphemes the Lord.

He says in his arrogance 'God will not avenge':
'There is no God' is all his thought.

---

[26] Quoted in *Relocations: the Churches' Report on Forced Removals,* South African Council of Churches and the Southern African Bishops' Conference, Johannesburg, 1984, p.8. Originally in the *Star,* Johannesburg, 14.6.83.

He is settled in all his ways:
your statutes, O Lord, are far above him,
   and he does not see.

He lies in wait to seize upon the poor:
he lays hold on the poor man
   and drags him off in his net.

The upright are crushed and humbled before him:
and the helpless fall into his power.

He says in his heart 'God has forgotten:
he has covered his face and sees nothing.'

The dark night

John de Gruchy

'If God is good and all powerful, why do the innocent suffer?' The question is universal, but it is more than a philosophical problem. Maria Zotwana's desolation is not academic, neither is that of the victims of the Holocaust or Hiroshima. The mysteries of suffering and of evil are theological issues, but they are even more experiences that defy reasoned debate. In the midst of cold dark emptiness we cannot break the silence with easy words, for they ring false and fail to comfort. Those in pain and anguish prefer the silence and the grasp of another's hand who has perhaps travelled that way before. If there is another. In the darkness we may come to firmer faith, many do, but many do not.

There is a different experience of darkness. Christian mystics speak of the 'dark night of the soul', that critical, humbling recurring stage through which we have to pass on the path to the true knowledge of God; a series of moments when the soul experiences God's presence as an absence. St John of the Cross describes it in this way: 'what the sorrowful soul feels most in this condition is its clear perception, as it thinks, that God has abandoned it, and, in his abhorrence of it, has flung it into darkness.'[27]

Such experiences have often been linked to the cry of

[27] St John of the Cross, *Dark Night of the Soul*, translated and edited by E. Allison Peers, Doubleday, New York, 1959, p.104.

dereliction uttered by Jesus on the cross. The Bible, especially the psalms and the writings of Job and Jeremiah, are full of these profoundly human experiences of being forsaken by God in the hour of greatest need. Nevertheless, in the Bible as in the writings of the mystics, this experience of absence is always qualified. God is not really absent, he has only hidden himself for a moment. The experience is one of testing, one of growth, one which will lead to the stronger affirmation and knowledge of God.

But there is another experience of deep darkness which does not lead to stronger faith but often to convinced atheism. Just over a century ago the German philosopher Friedrich Nietzsche proclaimed the death of God. 'God is dead. God remains dead. And we have killed him.' Nietzsche's personal journey from Christian faith to atheism is a particularly complex one, but it is not uncommon. The secularization of European culture, its scientific modernization, has been an experience of alienation from religious roots and belief in God. This is not a cheap atheism, the acceptance of an easy option not to believe because it is more convenient than to believe. It is a process of alienation in which estrangement is accepted with profound reluctance; belief would be preferred but not at the cost of honesty and integrity.

The experience of the absence of God has been aided by false theologies of power and privilege which, in the name of God, have supported war, racism and oppression. For this reason many can no longer believe in God. For them, God is dead and, more terrifyingly, our inhumanity towards others has killed him. This is not the mystics' 'dark night of the soul' experienced, perhaps, in the solitude of the monastery cell. It is a cultural shock, a social 'dark night' experienced in the midst of life as history unfolds before us, mere pawns in its grasp. This is not simply the experience of some intellectuals and philosophers. It is the experience of being socially uprooted and dumped in alien soil, the experience of millions of refugees and exiles the world over, the experience of victims incarcerated and tortured, the poor, defenceless peoples of the world whose cries to God seem unheard and unheeded. The absence of God experienced as the presence not only of suffering but even more, the presence of evil. For the victims, belief in God is not an intellectual exercise but the presence or absence of hope.

The lights go out
Mongane Serote[28]

Too much blood has been spilled
Please my countrymen, can someone say a word of wisdom
It is too late
Blood, no matter how little of it
when it spills on the brain —
on the memory of a nation
it is as if the sea floods the earth
The lights go out
mad hounds howl in the dark
Ah, we've become familiar with horror
the heart of our country
when it makes its pulse
ticking time
wounds us
My countrymen, can someone who understands that it is
now too late
who knows that exploitation and oppression are brains
which being
insane only know violence
can someone teach us how to mount the wound and fight.
The bright eye of the night keeps whispering and whispering
the shadows form and unfold
the trees hide in the dark
the grass whistles
the night is silent with experience
this night
in these parts of the world . . .
But,
no screams ring forever

---

[28] An extract from Mongane Serote, *The Night Keeps Winking*, Gaberone, Botswana, p.7.

nor does pain last forever
something will always be done
the night knows this
this night which makes a day . . .

Arise, O Lord

Psalm 10:13-20

Arise, O Lord God, lift up your hand:
forget not the poor for ever.

Why should the wicked man spurn God:
why should he say in his heart 'He will not avenge'?

Surely you see the trouble and the sorrow:
you look on, and will take it into your own hands.

The helpless commits himself to you:
for you are the helper of the fatherless.

Break the power of the ungodly:
search out his wickedness till it is found no more.

The Lord is king for ever and ever:
the heathen have perished from his land.

You have heard the longing of the meek, O Lord:
you turned your ear to their hearts' desire,

To help the poor and fatherless to their right:
that men may no more be terrified from their land.

Righteous Anger

The Christian life, aware of the pain, suffering and hurt experienced by others, is angered by that which destroys the lives and rights of people. The Bible speaks of the 'wrath of God', that is, God's anger towards sin because of its destructive consequences for human life and community. Righteous anger is not the seeking of vengeance, it is the awakening of a concern for truth, justice, and an expression of love.

The wrath of God

Psalm 76:7-12

Terrible are you, Lord God:
and who may stand before you when you are angry?

You caused your sentence to be heard from heaven:
the earth feared and was still

When God arose to judgement:
to save all the meek of the earth.

For you crushed the wrath of man;
you bridled the remnant of the wrathful.

O make vows to the Lord your God, and keep them:
let all around him bring gifts
to him that is worthy to be feared.

For he cuts down the fury of princes:
and he is terrible to the kings of the earth.

The anger of Christ
John 2:13-17 (JB)

Just before the Jewish Passover Jesus went up to Jerusalem, and in the Temple he found people selling cattle and sheep and pigeons, and the money changers sitting at their counters there. Making a whip out of some cord, he drove them all out of the Temple, cattle and sheep as well, scattered the money changers' coins, knocked their tables over and said to the pigeon-sellers, 'Take all this out of here and stop turning my Father's house into a market'. Then his disciples remembered the words of scripture: *Zeal for your house will devour me.*

An overwhelming feeling of anger
Francis Wilson

Towards the end of 1974 and for several months after, a large number of black student leaders were arrested and detained without trial by the South African security police. Some were held in solitary confinement for lengthy periods. All were finally released without being charged of any crime. During that period a Vigil of Prayer was held at St George's Cathedral, Cape Town. This reflection by Francis Wilson, professor of economics at the University of Cape Town, dated 13 February, 1975, is one of many that was written during the vigil by those who spent the allotted twenty-four hours in prayer for those detained. The name of one detainee was the focus for each session.[29]

I have been thinking of Menziwe Mbeo, a person I have never met but somebody about whom I have become conscious these past twelve hours. The notes in front of me do not tell us very much, they are no substitute for meeting and getting to know him. But they tell us enough. He is young, only 27. He was expelled from the University of Fort Hare. He was in Durban helping to organise a trade union for black workers. He was detained on 26 September 1974, so today is the 141st day of his incarceration. And what has been happening to him? We don't know. He has not been charged with any crime; not even the net of the Terrorism Act is wide

[29] I am indebted to Fr. David Russell who provided me with the three volumes of Vigil Reflections which are in his possession, and from which this reading and the Vigil prayer which follows are taken.

enough to enable the police to accuse him. But still they have the power to hold and, possibly, break him. I confess that my overwhelming feeling whilst I have been here and thought, read a prayer about the different people, has not been one of guilt for myself, nor even of sympathy for the detained and those whom they love, but rather one of anger. The whole thing is monstrous, outrageous, wicked, evil . . . words fail me. How dare the state, the security police, the white voters (of whom I am one), the authorities, or whoever it is act so viciously to destroy good men and women and their works.

As I read through the notes on the detainees I am struck by the fact that this is really a roll call of some of the finest, most sensitive, most articulate and most courageous of the young generation (almost all in their twenties) of black South Africans. Sure, one does not want to get all romantic and pretend that everybody is a saint, but who, reading this list, can deny that these are the young leaders, the idealists, not the criminals of black South Africa? I know Nyameko Barney Pityana who today is spending his 142nd day in God knows what circumstances. For such a man as he to be incarcerated is a judgment not upon Barney but upon the society which has acted so violently against him. So, then, I ask all my fellow vigil-keepers, as, indeed, I ask myself, are we angry enough? Are we angry not only because of what is being done to people, but also because of the justifications being used to do it — to maintain 'our Christian way of life?'

We are angry, yes. But is anger good? It seems to me that what is bad is the bitterness and violence that can flow from anger. But not all anger is bad — look at Jesus driving the merchants from the Temple. The bitterness comes, doesn't it, from anger combined with impotence. Too often we, the church, look at bitterness and tell people to stop being angry. I think that is wrong. We must focus rather on the impotence and ask how this can be transformed so that the anger itself can be a cleansing and renewing energy as it was in the case of our Lord.

But how is this impotence transformed? As one gropes for an answer it seems to me that part of the answer lies in prayer. That sounds very conventional and trite. Nevertheless I do believe that God gives sight to those who would see; that he cures the extraordinary blindness from which we all suffer in different aspects of our lives and personalities; that he grants the great gift of imagination if we will dare but ask him for it. And imagination is power. The helplessness and impotence which we so often feel arises because we do not know what to do, we cannot think of appropriate action. Yet if we can at least begin by praying regularly that God will show us, puny as we are, what we can do for the healing of our land, I am convinced that little by little over the years he will show us.

Our fellow prisoners

Hebrews 13:3 (NIV)

Remember those in prison as if you were their fellow prisoners, and those who are ill-treated as if you yourselves were suffering.

May anger and fear give way to love

A Vigil Prayer: Margaret Nash,
19 February 1975

Dr Margaret Nash is an ecumenical consultant and author engaged in ministry to the dispossessed.

O God
whose Son in anger
drove the money-changers
from the temple
let the anger of Nkwenkwe Nkomo
and his fellow detainees
be to the cleansing
of this land.

O God
I hold before you
the anger
the rage
the frustration
the sorrow

of Mrs Nkomo and all black mothers
who demand for their children
the same chance to grow up
strong and tall
loving and unafraid
as any white mother
wants for her children;

In penitence
I offer you
my own mixed up anger
that it, with theirs,
may be taken up
into your redemptive will
in which the clash
between anger and fear
oppressed and oppressor
can give way
to the incomprehensible action
of agape-love
bringing about the reconciliation
the embrace of the other
the alien
the enemy
creating the festival of shalom
in which the wolf shall lie down
with the lamb
and the whole of life on earth
shall rejoice
in the splendour of your glory.

14

The Rage for Justice

The Christian life is meant to be an expression of the love of God. Love is not sentimental, and when expressed in society it is 'a hunger to see right prevail'. The rage for justice is an expression of love for the neighbour.

Let justice roll on

Amos 5:18-24 (NIV)

Woe to you who long
for the day of the Lord!
Why do you long for the day of the Lord?
That day will be darkness, not light.
It will be as though a man had fled from a lion
only to meet a bear,
as though he entered his house
and rested his hand on the wall
only to have a snake bite him.
Will not the day of the Lord be darkness, not light —
pitch-dark, without a ray of brightness?

I hate, I despise your religious feasts;
I cannot stand your assemblies.
Even though you bring me burnt offerings
and grain offerings,
I will not accept them.
Though you bring choice fellowship offerings,
I will have no regard for them.

Away with the noise of your songs!
I will not listen to the music of your harps.
But let justice roll on like a river,
righteousness like a never-failing stream!

Choose justice
Monica Wilson[30]

The rage for justice keeps seizing men and women. People
ask why students are restless: why housewives spend hours
standing holding placards: this is why. In the very contra-
dictions of the society, such as between torture and
concentration camps, and the hungering and thirsting after
righteousness and justice, lies the room for choice. The
essence of Christian teaching is that there is a choice in our
lives; that the Spirit leads us in discerning choice.

Some behaviourists try to persuade us that there is no
such thing as choice; that everything that a man does is
determined by his heredity and environment; that he has no
freedom whatever; choice is an illusion. But I have yet to
meet a behaviourist who did not himself choose; who really
believed that he had no choice whatsoever in whom he
should marry or what sort of work he should do. I do not find
Marxists who believe in dialectical determinism leaving the
determinism to work itself out, any more than Christians
who really believe in the coming of the kingdom sit back and
let it come. I would go further and argue that with the
increasing of society choice expands; we, in a large society,
are less bound by material necessity than those living very
isolated lives. And the more talented a man or woman is the
greater the choices before them. John Taylor argues that the
Spirit 'creates occasions for choice'. Again the gospel is clear
about the obligations of the talented to choose.

One of the functions of the church is to help people to
choose. Many are confused by the very wealth of choice
before them: the set patterns of a more static period of

[30] Monica Wilson, 'The Future of Christian Churches in South Africa', *Journal of
Theology for Southern Africa*, no. 12, September 1975, pp.13-15. Monica Wilson was Professor of Social Anthropology at the University of Cape Town.

history are no longer there and continually we have to adjust to a new sort of society. Adjusting means choosing and people lose their nerve.

If the Church is indeed the embodiment of faith, it teaches us to go out into the unknown. 'By faith Abraham, when he was called to go out into a place which he should after receive for an inheritance, obeyed.' Our fathers acted on faith when they set sail for an unknown land. I think of J.T. van der Kemp, Joseph Williams, John Philip, John Brownlee, John Bennie, John Ayliff, William Shaw, Henry Dugmore. The first black Christians walked by faith: men like Ntsikana, Tiyo Soga and his mother, John Knox Bokwe, Elijah Makiwane, Mpambane Mzimba . . . it is a splendid roll. Some of what our fathers built has been destroyed, but the faith they taught is resurrected in new forms. The very conflicts of the frontier offered to our fathers an opportunity for creation, and this is what I, as a South African, hold on to now.

The conflicts of our society compel change, and the Holy Spirit can lead us in choosing what sort of change it will be in creating a new sort of society. Anthony Barker talks of the 'theft of hope' as the very worst thing that white has brought upon black, and the temptation to despair lurks all around. It is the function of the church to prophesy, by which I understand to make people face the facts of our situation and the judgment of God upon it; to face the implications of continuing separation of husbands and wives; of removals of people; of exclusion from the common life of the community; of desperate poverty in the midst of plenty. The challenge to create something different is the future of the Christian church in South Africa.

All I want is justice

Jill King[31]

I had this job, see,
in the Bantu Labour Offices.
Those people, slow's the word,
and all busy dodging the rules.
Anyone'd think the Homelands
were pestilent. Only interested
in raking in the highest wages.
And the women — dead set on the city.

Well, I died. Shock, that.
No time even to draw my pension
(which was the main reason I joined).
At the gate Peter stood;
didn't wave me on, like I was expecting.
After all, haven't I done my best,
been a good husband, worked for the kids,
kept my home going?
He read out from his book,
I tell you I didn't like his tone:
'You have separated
wives from their husbands,
torn homes apart, taken men's work away from them,
sent exiles to a far country.'
Me! I ask you!
'All I did, Sir,
was to carry out orders
as decently as possible.'

But he'd gone, leaving me this form —
Permit to stay in area refused.
ENDORSED OUT.

I'm taking it up
with a higher authority.

---

[31] First published in the Woman's Argus, Cape Town, 16.11.72. Reprinted in *Pro Veritate*, 15 April 1973.

I am not prepared to concede
Trevor Huddleston CR[32]

Bishop Huddleston is retired bishop of Stepney and leader in the anti-apartheid movement. During 1944-56 Fr. Huddleston was a parish priest in Sophiatown, a black township near Johannesburg. Towards the end of his ministry, the Sophiatown community was uprooted by the government and moved to the newly established Soweto township. Fr. Huddleston's book Naught for your Comfort *was based on his experiences within Sophiatown.*

In opposing the policies of the present Government I am not prepared to concede that any momentary good which might conceivably emerge from them is good. Nor am I prepared to concede that the motives which inspire such policies have any quality of goodness about them. For both the acts and the motives are inspired by a desire which is itself fundamentally evil and basically un-Christian: the desire to dominate in order to preserve a position of racial superiority, and in that process of domination to destroy personal relationships, the foundation of love itself. That is anti-Christ.

If I am mistaken, as well I may be, in the methods I have used: then I trust in the mercy of God for my forgiveness. For he, too, is a person. And it is his person that I have found in Africa, in the poverty of her homes, in the beauty and splendour of her children, in the patience and courtesy of her people. But above all, I have found him where every Christian should expect to find him: in the darkness, in the fear, in the blinding weariness of Calvary.

And Calvary is but one step from the Empty Tomb.

---

[32] Trevor Huddleston CR, *Naught for Your Comfort*, Collins, London 1956.

The sun of justice is risen

Violine Cebani[33]

Alleluia, alleluia, alleluia, alleluia.
Alleluia, alleluia, alleluia, alleluia.

The Sun of Justice is risen, he is risen as he said.
The Light shines into the prison, he is risen as he said.
Alleluia . . .

Liberty to the captives, new sight to the blind,
Good news for the poor, a new dawn for humankind.
Alleluia . . .

from the Xhosa

[33] Composed by Violine Cebani in Xhosa under the title 'Mafu Zulu', and translated by Fr. Dave Dargie.

15

Liberation from Bondage

The Christian life witnesses to the purpose of God that all people should be free from the shackles which enslave, degrade, and dehumanize. The Christian cannot stand by, or pass by on the other side, when people are treated unjustly or kept in bondage by the pride, selfishness and greed of others.

Let my people go
Exodus 6:1-11 (NIV)

Then the Lord said to Moses, 'Now you will see what I will do to Pharoah: Because of my mighty hand he will let them go; because of my mighty hand he will drive them out of his country.' God also said to Moses, 'I am the Lord. I appeared to Abraham, to Isaac and to Jacob as God Almighty, but by my name the Lord I did not make myself known to them. I also established my covenant with them to give them the land of Canaan, where they lived as aliens. Moreover, I have heard the groaning of the Israelites, whom the Egyptians are enslaving, and I have rememberd my covenant. Therefore, say to the Israelites: 'I am the Lord and I will bring you out from under the yoke of the Egyptians. I will free you from being slaves to them and will redeem you with an out-stretched arm and with mighty acts of judgment. I will take you as my own people, and I will be your God. Then you will know that I am the Lord your God, who brought you out from under the the yoke of the Egyptians. And I will bring you to the land that I swore with uplifted hand to give to

Abraham, to Isaac and to Jacob. I will give it to you as a possession. I am the Lord. Moses reported this to the Israelites, but they would not listen to him because of their discouragement and cruel bondage. Then the Lord said to Moses, 'Go, tell Pharaoh king of Egypt to let the Israelites go out of his country.'

Liberty for the oppressed
Luke 4:14-21 (RSV)

And Jesus returned in the power of the Spirit into Galilee, and a report concerning him went out through all the surrounding country. And he taught in their synagogues, being glorified by all. And he came to Nazareth, where he had been brought up; and he went to the synagogue, as his custom was, on the sabbath day. And he stood up to read; and there was given to him the book of the prophet Isaiah. He opened the book and found the place where it was written,

The Spirit of the Lord is upon me,
because he has anointed me to preach good news to the poor.
He has sent me to proclaim release to the captives
and recovering of sight to the blind,
to set at liberty those who are oppressed,
to proclaim the acceptable year of the Lord.

And he closed the book, and gave it back to the attendant, and sat down; and the eyes of all in the synagogue were fixed on him. And he began to say to them, 'Today this scripture has been fulfilled in your hearing.'

The liberation of the cross
Pastor Z. Kameeta[34]

God be praised, Jesus did not carry out only half of God's commission to liberate the world, but steadfastly went on to its completion, even the cross. God be praised, Jesus did not get down from the cross, he did not leave the field before the deciding battle could be fought. He stood firm until he had

[34] Edited extracts from an unpublished sermon preached in Afrikaans by Pastor Kameeta of the Evangelical Lutheran Church at a meeting of the Namibia National Convention on Easter Sunday, 1976.

Liberation from bondage

won the victory and so confirmed once and for ever the reality of God's liberating will in this world. God be praised for leaving him there to accept me. He went through hell to bring me out of there.

May the name of the Lord be praised because his cry from the cross is the fulfilment of God's promise of salvation. Each punch in the face, each mocking word, each blow of the hammer mercilessly driving the nails through his hands was a determined step towards his goal, the liberation of the world. His suffering was not an end in itself, his aim was the liberation of the whole creation and the establishment of God's rule in this world. That is the rule of truth and peace. No peace, peace imposed by armoured cars, batons, guns and dogs, but that peace which like a clear stream flows from the inexhaustible spring of God's love, from self-surrender and service to God and neighbour.

Those who love this truth, justice and peace, follow in these determined footsteps of Christ to liberation. Each restriction or banishment they endure, each cuff or kick, each day in the cells of loneliness, each electrical shock, each barbaric method suffered to give false testimony, each humiliation, each death in detention, each tear shed in this fight against evil for the sake of peace, truth and justice, is a determined step forward in the footsteps of our Hero and Victor. Through all this wrongdoing the structure of oppression places itself under the judgment of God. All these deeds done in the hope of self-preservation are deeds of self-destruction. The tension of this battle here on Golgotha is so great it takes one's breath away. The revolution which it brings about is incomparable, it is deep and comprehensive. It changes both hearts and structures.

The events of Golgotha did not take place in a vacuum but in the midst of the crowd which cried out 'Crucify him!' It took place in this world which hates the truth and prefers the lie, rejects unity and sees division as ideal. The battle of Golgotha was felt not only by those who stood around the cross or in the temple, but by the whole creation. And God has, through the cross, made peace with us, heaven and earth have been reconciled. The wall of enmity which we ourselves erected between God and ourselves has been cast down by the violence of the cross, and the walls which separate us from one another have also been cast down. This is the revolution of the cross. This is the deep and all-embracing revolution that is not restricted to the altar or pulpit but extends through the whole of history, through powers and structures of injustice, oppression and exploitation. Every system and government which builds up these separating walls is confronted by the revolution of the cross. A revolution which goes deep, converting the heart and the whole personality. And those who are converted are used by God himself as agents of liberation, to cast down the powers, structures and governments which build these walls, by the word of the cross, the sword of the Spirit.

This is what the gospel is about. It tells us what God has done through his Son, Jesus Christ. Our guilt is washed away if we believe in him and we are converted. This is a painful process, an indescribable challenge. In this conversion I am torn free of the life of injustice, hatred, exploitation and racism. This leaves bleeding wounds behind — that is why we fear conversion and flee from the face of God and his Word.

My fellows in oppression, strangers in your own country, return to the Lord! You cannot effectively work and struggle for liberation if you yourselves are living like that against which you struggle. So come back to him who is the liberator of Israel. Never cease, by word and deed, to carry the gospel of liberation and reconciliation into the world, especially to those who oppress and persecute us.

Freedom via the cross
Albert Luthuli[35]

These are the concluding paragraphs from Nobel Peace Prize winner, Chief Albert Luthuli's statement after he was dismissed from his position as Chief by the South African government in November 1952. Chief Luthuli, a deacon in the Congregational Church at Groutville,

[35] Albert Luthuli, *Let my People Go*, Collins, London, 1962, p.238.

Natal, was leader of the African National Congress when it was banned in 1961.

As for myself, with a full sense of responsibility and clear conviction, I decided to remain in the struggle for extending democratic rights and responsibilities to all sections of the South African community. I have embraced the non-Violent Passive Resistance technique in fighting for freedom because I am convinced it is the only non-revolutionary, legitimate and human way that could be used by people denied, as we are, effective constitutional means to further aspirations. The wisdom or foolishness of this decision I place in the hands of the Almighty.

What the future has in store for me I do not know. It might be ridicule, imprisonment, concentration camp, flogging, banishment and even death. I only pray to the Almighty to strengthen my resolve so that none of these grim possibilities may deter me from striving, for the sake of the good name of our beloved country, South Africa, to make it a true democracy and a true union in form and spirit of all the communities in the land.

My only painful concern at times is that of the welfare of my family but I try even in this regard, in a spirit of trust and surrender to God's will as I see it, to say 'God will provide.'

It is inevitable that in working for Freedom some individuals and some families must take the lead and suffer: the Road to Freedom is via the Cross. *Mayibuye! Afrika!*

Come, freedom, come!

Walter M.B. Nhlapo[36]

Rising in the morn I cry
'Come Freedom today!'
At midday I sit and sigh,
'When comes the great day?'
God! To Thee I bring my sorrow,
Tears I daily weep;

---

[36] Walter M.B. Nhlapo, 'Come, Freedom, Come', first published in *The Voice*, July 1950. *The Return of the Aamasi Bird*, p.157.

Must they be my food tomorrow?
If so, give me sleep!

A litany for the world we live in

Prayers prepared by the Algoa Regional Council (Eastern Cape) of the United Congregational Church for Ascension Day, 1985, following the tragic police killings of blacks in Uitenhage and elsewhere in the Eastern Cape a few weeks earlier.

Leader: For exploiter and exploited; for persecutor and persecuted; for oppressor and oppressed; for criminal and victim, God of perfect love, we pray.

People: As we pray, remove the fear that makes us strident and vengeful, and take away the woolliness of thought that makes us sentimental.

Leader: Give us clear eyes to see the world as it is and ourselves and all people as we are; but give us hope to go on believing in the possibility of what you intend all of us to be.

People: We pray for children growing up with no sense of beauty, no feeling for what is good or bad, no knowledge of you and your love in Christ.

Leader: We pray for men and women who have lost faith and given up hope; for governments who crush people's spirits, and for governments slow to act in the cause of justice, freedom and development.

People: We pray for the whole church and the world, giving thanks for your goodness, for your love, made known in Christ, for your truth confirmed in his death and resurrection, for your promises to us and to all people, keeping hope alive in spite of our failure and rebellion.

People: Let us go to our work and into our relationships stimulated by hope, strengthened by faith, directed by love, to play our part in the liberation of all people, in the name of Jesus Christ our Lord.

When justice and peace kiss composed by Student's Union for
Christian Action, based on Psalm 85:10

When love and faithfulness come together
And righteousness and peace join hands
When peace and justice kiss one another
Then freedom will come to our land.
Then freedom will come to our land,
Then freedom will come to our land
When peace and justice kiss one another
And with righteousness join hands.

When love and faithfulness come together
And righteousness and peace embrace
When peace and justice kiss one another
With new hope the future we'll face
With new hope the future we'll face,
With new hope the future we'll face
When peace and justice kiss one another
And with righteousness embrace.

16

Spirituality of the Kingdom

The Christian life is lived under the reign of God revealed in Jesus Christ. It is life lived in the expectation that God's reign will be fully established at the end of the age in the second advent of Christ. Then true peace and justice will finally flourish among the nations. Until then, the Christian lives between the times, witnessing to and praying for the coming of God's kingdom 'on earth as it is in heaven'.

The future reign of God
Daniel 7:13-14 (JB)

I gazed into the visions of the night.
And I saw, coming on the clouds of heaven,
one like a son of man.
He came to the one of great age
and was led into his presence.
On him was conferred sovereignty,
glory and kingship,
and men of all peoples, nations and languages
became his servants.
His sovereignty is an eternal sovereignty
which shall never pass away,
nor will his empire ever be destroyed.

The kingdom of God is near
Mark 1:14-18 (NIV)

After John was put in prison, Jesus went into Galilee proclaiming the good news of God. 'The time has come,' he said.

'The kingdom of God is near. Repent and believe the good news!'

As Jesus walked beside the Sea of Galilee, he saw Simon and his brother Andrew casting a net into the lake, for they were fishermen. 'Come, follow me,' Jesus said, 'and I will make you fishers of men.' At once they left their nets and followed him.

Signs of the times   Matthew 24:3-14 (NIV)

As Jesus was sitting on the Mount of Olives, the disciples came to him privately. 'Tell us,' they said, 'when will this happen, and what will be the sign of your coming and of the end of the age?'

Jesus answered: 'Watch out that no one deceives you. For many will come in my name, claiming, 'I am the Christ,' and will deceive many. You will hear of wars and rumours of wars, but see to it that you are not alarmed. Such things must happen, but the end is still to come. Nation will rise against nation, and kingdom against kingdom. There will be famines and earthquakes in various places. All these are the beginning of birth-pains.

'Then you will be handed over to be persecuted and put to death, and you will be hated by all nations because of me. At that time many will turn away from the faith and will betray and hate each other, and many false prophets will appear and deceive many people. Because of the increase of wickedness, the love of most will grow cold, but he who stands firm to the end will be saved. And this gospel of the kingdom will be preached in the whole world as a testimony to all nations, and then the end will come.'

Experiencing the kingdom as near   Albert Nolan[37]

The conversion we all need to go through if we want to deepen our spiritual lives is a conversion to, a turning towards, the kingdom of God. The kingdom must become

---

[37] From Albert Nolan OP, *Biblical Spirituality*, Order of Preachers, Springs 1982, p.46f. Fr. Albert Nolan is a Dominican priest living and working in Johannesburg.

the most important reality in our lives, it must become the future event that determines and defines the whole meaning of our existence here and now. If we can learn to gear everything we do and say to the kingdom and if we try to understand everything that happens in the world in terms of the kingdom, then our lives will be transformed and the quality of everything we do will be changed. This is what the spiritual writers mean when they say that we should live *sub specie aeternitatis*.

But how do we do this? By reading the signs of the times, by becoming critical of the world we now experience and by coming to experience this present world as *unreal, inhuman, unloving* and totally *false*. The kingdom is the opposite of all that is wrong and false in our world. Until we become fully aware of how wrong the world is and what exactly is wrong with it, we will never really appreciate the urgent need for God's kingdom of justice and peace.

Moreover, as we prayerfully try to read the signs of the times we will also begin to discover the *seeds* of God's kingdom as they manifest themselves in the midst of all the rot. The kingdom is basically a future event but we can find in ourselves and in the world today some seeds of the kingdom, some signs of the kingdom, some partial realisation of the kingdom. The Spirit of God is at work in the midst of all the falsehood and cruelty. You will find the values of the kingdom being lived out by some people and you will find the kingdom in the hearts of those who really believe in it and hope for it. Gradually the kingdom can become a reality for us, a reality that dominates our lives and concerns as it did for Jesus.

The kingdom model   Cedric Mayson[38]

On the cross he discarded the cosmic powers and authorities like a garment; he made a public spectacle of them and led them as captives in his triumphal procession (Colossians 2:15).

---

[38] An extract from an editorial in *Pro Veritate*, April 1976. Cedric Mayson, a Methodist minister, was a staff member of the Christian Institute and editor of *Pro Veritate* before they were banned in 1977.

What, then, is the sequel to Jesus' exposé of society on the cross? The traumatic power in Christ runs from the cross into the resurrection and we might expect him to form either a 'pure' religion or a 'pure' political system for God's kingdom to come. He does neither. He establishes a model out of which God's kingdom might develop, and that model is not based on policies and systems but on personal relationships.

The kingdom-model starts with the intimate friendship between Jesus and people, and people and people: Mary, Peter, John, Thomas, the disciples, the believers; the followers; the in-group. These groups arise in normal places and events: in the home, by the beach, on the mountains; people working, eating, relaxing, discussing, fearing, doubting, trusting, living. As they seek to relate to one another in love the power to do so is given to them. They discover an honesty, a vision, a hope, a peace, a love that changes their whole approach to living. The Spirit that was in Jesus operates in them.

These groups grew a different life-style which began to enact the human realities of the kingdom of God, not from a policy-decision, but out of the power discovered in themselves. The study of the teachings of Jesus were central to them, and they gave a strong place to the spiritual necessities of human beings. They shared a common life according to the material resources and needs of each one, including the sharing of meals and possessions. The racial and religious barriers between Jew and Greek, the economic and class barriers between slave and freeman, and the barriers which parted men and women were conquered. Their style of life was transformed and transforming.

The implications of the new life brought challenges and these were resolved not by referring to a statement, but in the crucible of their experience of being real human beings in Christ. Heresy was not judged against a creed or manifesto, but against their joint experience of living amongst those with the simple faith: 'Jesus is Lord.'

It was this joyful, unconscious enactment of the kingly rule of God that produced an immediate impact on the religious, economic, political and social world around them. Their life style in Christ started changing their society. This was the pattern of the first followers of the Way; it has been the pattern in every age of renewal. It is the pattern we must rediscover today.

May the love of Christ transform us   Douglas Bax

O Lord,
we can never fully comprehend
the length, breadth, depth and height of your love:
but we pray that that love may so transform us
through your suffering
as to make us reach out to
the despairing and the desperate
and work for peace and reconciliation between all people.
For Jesus' sake hear our prayer.   Amen

Kingdom prayer   Matthew 6:9-13 (NIV)

Our Father in heaven,
hallowed be your name,
your kingdom come,
your will be done
on earth as it is in heaven.
Give us today our daily bread.
Forgive us our debts,
as we also have forgiven our debtors.
And lead us not into temptation,
but deliver us from evil.

An acclamation   Revelation 11:15 (NIV)

The kingdom of the world
has become the kingdom of our Lord
and of his Christ,
and he will reign for ever and ever.

God and the National Interest

The Christian life owes its primary allegiance to the kingdom of God. The Christian is called to pray for those in authority and to seek the welfare of the country. In some contexts, however, even worship and prayer can be regarded as acts of civil disobedience.

Prayer as civil disobedience
Daniel 6:10-16 (NIV)

Now when Daniel learned that the decree had been published, he went home to his upstairs room where the windows opened toward Jerusalem. Three times a day he got down on his knees and prayed, giving thanks to his God, just as he had done before. Then these men went as a group and found Daniel praying and asking God for help. So they went to the king and spoke to him about his royal decree: 'Did you not publish a decree that during the next thirty days anyone who prays to any god or man except to you, O king, would be thrown into the lions' den?' The king answered, 'The decree stands — in accordance with the laws of the Medes and Persians, which cannot be annulled.' Then they said to the king, 'Daniel, who is one of the exiles from Judah, pays no attention to you, O king, or to the decree you put in writing. He still prays three times a day.' When the king heard this, he was greatly distressed; he was determined to rescue Daniel and made every effort until sundown to save him. Then the men went as a group to the king and said to him, 'Remember, O king, that according to the law of the

Medes and Persians no decree or edict that the king issues can be changed.' So the king gave the order, and they brought Daniel into the lions' den. The king said to Daniel, 'May your God, whom you serve continually, rescue you!'

God on approval

John Davies[39]

Some of the most significant occasions of history have been when a small group of people stuck out for what they knew to be true and right; we think of such minorities as the French Resistance and the anti-Nazi Confessing Church in Germany in recent years, back to the small groups of Christians in the days of persecution, facing emperors as gladiators.

The book of Daniel was written for such a group, a little group which at the time must have looked doomed to an obscure and unremembered destruction. It tells of a good man who is prepared to be entirely alone because of his complete commitment to the truth. In the story of Daniel and the Den of Lions, all the forces of law and of the police are brought unjustly against him, and he wins.

The question at issue was the central question of religion and politics, 'Who is God?' Is God the national advantage, political unity, a community principle, an ethnic symbol? Or, is God the universal authority of heaven and earth? Who or what is your God? And, maybe more important, who or what decides who or what is God? Who or what decides what shall be of supreme value and significance?

In Daniel's situation, the politicians took it upon themselves to decide. 'We decide', they said, 'that the supreme national interest will be God — we will pray to the central symbol of our ethnic inheritance — in a word, the king. We will arrange for him to be God and to have all the prestige of God. We will have a God who will be of our own choice, devised for our national advantage, limited to our interests, guaranteed by our support. We will make this king God for

---

[39] From John Davies, 'Lions' Den and Christ's Grave', *Pro Veritate*, 15 November 1968, pp.15-16. John Davies was Anglican Chaplain at the University of the Witwatersrand, Johannesburg, during the nineteen-sixties.

ourselves, for an experimental period of thirty days; we will have God on approval, so that we can see how it works; and we will give the law a magical authority to ensure that this God be God; we cannot be sure that a God of our own devising is really God, so we will bring in lots of extra legislation to make up for the weakness of our ideological position'.

The politicians do this because they know that the ordinary legal processes will serve only to expose the righteousness of the honest man; they know that he is not going to be vulnerable to any accusation unless commitment to the true God is made a criminal offence; and so the law has to be manipulated in order to be the instrument of the honest man's downfall. So they find themselves making a law against God; for the true God they substitute another God, a God who is for *us* over against *them*, a God who stands or falls with our national identity, a God who can be located in our ethnic group, a God who can give us security by his power to get people who are unlike us moved out. For it was not Daniel's wisdom or skill that made him unacceptable; it was simply that he was of the wrong ethnic and cultural inheritance. It was this that caused all this trouble and idolatry, and abrogation of law.

And Daniel's reaction? He does not protest, he does not propose resolutions at synod, he does not even produce a theological manifesto. He calmly and deliberately commits an overt act of civil disobedience. And the king, who benefits from all the glamour and prestige of his status as God, realises too late that you cannot have this except at someone else's expense. There comes a time when kindness and charity are not enough. There comes a time when praying is not enough. The king is desperately sad at the unjust treatment of Daniel; he makes all sorts of deploring noises about Daniel's enforced removal; he loses a night's sleep on account of Daniel's ideological punishment. But it is *too late*, because the fault is already in the structure, and he is powerless to alter it; it is *too late*, because the fault is in a community that has sacrificed truth and justice to its desire for ethnic purity and sectional security; it is *too late*, because the king himself has allowed his interests and his security to be given supreme value over the values of the one true God who is for all.

And help, if there is help at all, has to come from a different source. The political leaders are wholly committed to a course of subversion of the principles of law and are jealous for their policies; the king himself is trapped in a system which he did not particularly want but which he did not have the motivation to reject. Help, if there is help at all, must come from the very one who has been rejected and discarded, the God of the rejected and discarded Daniel. Neither politicians nor king can stop the mouths of lions. But the supreme God, who made both politicians and kings and lions, can do so. Lions can be brought to accept his authority; and so must kings and politicians. Only in this God, only in the God who is for all people, nations, and languages, only in the one God whose gifts of justice and righteousness, of peace and security, are for all people, only in this one true God is the salvation which can operate to save the individual from the unjust system and its unjust administrators.

Let us be clear about this claim. When we stand as Christians for the claims of God, we are not just saying, 'Our God is better than yours, or stronger or wiser than yours'. We are not entering an ideological competition. The question is whether we stand for something sectional or something universal. The sectional power always regards the outsider as a rival, as someone to dissociate from: the universal always regards the outsider as one with whom we are being brought into association by the power of God. The sectional seeks to emphasise and underline the outsider's identification as an outsider: the universal seeks to overcome the barrier which identifies the outsider as outsider. The sectional identifies the structures of religion as 'our'; the universal sees that all is God's. There is only a very short step from talking about *our* churches, *our* pulpits, *our* denomination, to talking about *our* God. If we control *our* church, if we decide who can come in and who cannot, if we use it to support *our* group identity, very soon God will be just *our* God, kept in business by us, supported by us, maintained by us. And the true God, who was for Daniel, will be against us.

Prayer of Petition[40]

This day O God of mercy
we bring before you all those
who suffer in prison,
who are oppressed,
who mourn those who die in freedom struggles;
in places like Soweto, Crossroads, Uitenhage, Sharpeville
and many places not known to us.
Deliver us from the chains of apartheid,
bring us all to the true liberty
of the Sons and Daughters of God.
Confound the ruthless
and grant us the power of your kingdom.

Acclamation

Revelation 5:6, 12-14 (NIV)

Then I saw a Lamb, looking as if it had been slain, standing in the centre of the throne, encircled by four living creatures and the elders. And they sang a new song:

> You are worthy to take the scroll
> and open its seals,
> because you were slain,
> and with your blood you purchased men
> for God
> from every tribe and language
> and people and nation.
> You have made them to be a kingdom and
> priests to serve our God,
> and they will reign on earth.
>
> Worthy is the Lamb, who was slain,
> to receive power and wealth and
> wisdom and strength
> and honour and glory and praise!

---

[40] Prayer used in the 16 June 1985 Prayer Service for the end of unjust rule, under the auspices of the Western Province Council of Churches.

Then I heard every creature in heaven and on earth and under the earth and on the sea, and all that is in them, singing:

> To him who sits on the throne
> and to the Lamb
> be praise and honour and glory and power
> for ever and ever! AMEN

The Great Amen

Arranged by S.C. Molefe[41]

Zulu
Asithi — Amen, siyakudumisa,
Asithi — Amen, siyakudumisa,
Asithi — Amen, Baba, Amen, Baba,
Amen, siyakudumisa.

Amen, amen — Amen, praise the name of the Lord,
Amen, amen — Amen, praise the name of the Lord,
Amen, amen — Amen, amen, Amen, amen,
Amen, praise the name of the Lord.

---

[41] In the *Lumko Song Book*, English translation and musical arrangement by Dave Dargie.

Living in Hope

The Christian life is one of hoping against hope. The Christian refuses to accept that things need be as they are: that there are no further possibilities; that all is ultimately meaningless; that there is no point to the struggle for what is right and just. The Christian is fully aware of the sinful brokenness of the human community, therefore Christian hope is not optimism, it is not living in an unrealistic world of wishful thinking. But despite so much evidence to the contrary, the Christian refuses to surrender hope and become cynical about the future of the world, precisely because it is God's world.

In this hope we were saved
Romans 8:18-25 (NIV)

I consider that our present sufferings are not worth comparing with the glory that shall be revealed in us. The creation waits in eager expectation for the sons of God to be revealed. For the creation was subjected to frustration, not by its own choice, but by the will of the one who subjected it, in hope that the creation itself will be liberated from its bondage to decay and brought into the glorious freedom of the children of God. We know that the whole creation has been groaning as in the pains of childbirth right up to the present time. Not only so, but we ourselves, who have the first fruits of the Spirit, groan inwardly as we wait eagerly for our adoption as sons, the redemption of our bodies. For in this hope we were saved. But hope that is seen is no hope at all. Who hopes for what he already has? But if we hope for what we do not yet have, we wait for it patiently.

An agony

Joyce Nomafa Sikakane[42]

My head is heavy, my shoulders shrug,
because despite
all my eyes have seen
my head has said
my heart has felt,
I do not believe
that White, Black and Yellow
cannot talk, walk, eat, kiss and share.
It worries me to think
that only people of my colour
will liberate me.

You mustn't trust a White man
my grandfather used to tell me
when I was a child.
You mustn't think that a White man cares for you
my people caution me.
You know when a White man wants to know you?
When you bring him money!

The Indian? He's black as you.
But, not as poor as you.
He knows his trade — cheating you.
He's happy to lend you money
just forgets to mention
the twenty per cent interest!
Until you have to pay it.

And the Coloured? I ask.
Ag! him, they say.
He doesn't know where he stands,
but, he prefers his skin whitest
and his hair straightest.
And somehow forgets the second names
of his black and kinky cousins!

[42] Joyce Nomafa Sikakane, 'An Agony', first published in *The Classic*, 1968. *The Return of the Aamasi Bird*, p.200f.

I know of Whites, Coloureds and Indians
who are like that, I say.
But, I'm told they are only a few.

Now, what about you my fellow African?
We are intimidated, they say,
Modimo, we're very very busy, they say,

not losing
our passes,
our birth certificates,
our train tickets,
our rent receipts,
our urban residential permits,
(not to mention our money, our husbands and
our lives).

My head is heavy, my shoulders shrug,
because despite
all my eyes have seen
my head has said
my heart has felt,
I do not believe
that White, Black and Yellow
cannot talk, walk, eat, kiss and share.

An ethic of hope

Manas Buthelezi[43]

The Christian gospel is designed to fill us with hope in order
that we may realise that life is worth living and that we have
a role to play in improving the quality of life of our fellows,
that is, filling them with the same hope that sustains us.
Hope is inseparable from faith and love (1 Corinthians
13:13). The dynamics of the Christian life are such that it is
almost impossible to determine with any degree of precision
where hope ends and where faith and love begin.

[43] An edited extract from Manas Buthelezi, 'Theological Grounds for an Ethic of Hope', in Basil Moore, (ed.) *Essays in Black Theology*, John Knox, Atlanta, 1974. Dr. Manas Buthelezi is a Bishop of the Evangelical Lutheran Church of Southern Africa and President of the South African Council of Churches.

The reality of sin that engulfs us in our sociality accounts for our conscious or subconscious experience of anxiety and estrangement. We are torn within ourselves and from our relationship with God and our fellows. This state of alienation creates within us a feeling of insecurity. Augustine underlined this truth when he remarked that our hearts are restless until they find their rest in God. But our restlessness takes many directions including the creation of human anchors of security. If we delay in finding the true God on whom to pin our hope, we do not hesitate to create gods after our own image. To speak of a society of hopeless people is a contradiction in terms for hopelessness and social order are mutually exclusive concepts. Hopelessness as the loss of a wholesome vision for what is and is to be is a sure gateway to anxiety and panic.

The Christian ethic is essentially an ethic of hope. The struggle against oppression coexists with the anticipation of victory as an event already realised. This is why delay in the manifestation of fruits does not detract from the intensity of a genuinely Christian ethical endeavour. The boundary between faith and hope melts away, for while faith affirms the reality of the present, hope affirms the future reality which is already certain. To know that God in Christ, who has called us to follow him under all circumstances, is also Lord over every situation breeds a sustaining hope.

Seen from the perspective of the sovereignty of God life cannot be separated into different compartments. We have the responsibility of inspiring hope not only among those who are struggling in the church, but also among those who are toiling in life situations which are ordinarily not regarded as Christian. Time and again the Christian tries, very often with apparent success, to run away from the hard and harsh realities of daily life in order to recoil into his spiritual and ecclesiastical ghetto. But this is impossible for we cannot escape our solidarity with others, including non-believers. In the arena of daily life the Christian needs a hope that will sustain him alongside his unbelieving brothers.

The gospel of hope for the condemned sinner cannot be fully grasped apart from an ethic of hope for social victims.

Wherein lies the hope of a poor person assuming that he or she also believes in Christ? In charity? Shall the poor continue in poverty so that charity may abound? God forbid. How can so highly-priced a love feed on human victims?

Our ethical responsibility is not only to serve others by removing the symptoms of alienation from the wholeness of life, but to equip them with the tools which will enable them to stand on their own feet. In this way we will be instilling in them courage to be themselves so that they may take their place at a point in life where God continuously gives gifts to his children. They will begin to have faith in themselves as human beings after we have had faith in them as our fellows, after we have accepted them as fellow-participants in the wholeness of life. We shall then all have something to live for, a hope that life is worth living. This is no utopian dream since it is part and parcel of the ethic of Jesus who ministered to the whole person and said to the paralytic 'Take heart, my child; your sins are forgiven'.

A Message of Hope   The Kairos Document[44]

Towards the end of September 1985 a group of black and white theologians, both professional and lay, living and working within the black townships around Johannesburg, produced a theological comment on the political crisis in South Africa. It has since been endorsed by many other theologians as well. Entitled Challenge to the Church: The Kairos Document, *it embodies one of the most rigorous and radical statements of the meaning and implications of the Christian faith to be published in South Africa. The following is an extract from chapter four, 'Towards a Prophetic Theology.'*

At the very heart of the gospel of Jesus Christ and at the centre of all true prophecy is a message of hope. Nothing could be more relevant and more necessary at this moment of crisis in South Africa than the Christian message of hope. As the crisis deepens day-by-day, what both the oppressor and the oppressed can legitimately demand of the churches

---

[44] Published by the Kairos Theologians, Braamfontein.

is a message of hope. Most of the oppressed people in South Africa today and especially the youth do have hope. They are acting courageously and fearlessly because they have a sure hope that liberation will come. Often enough their bodies are broken but nothing can now break their spirit. But hope needs to be confirmed. Hope needs to be maintained and strengthened. Hope needs to be spread. The people need to hear it said again and again that God is with them.

On the other hand the oppressor and those who believe the propaganda of the oppressor are desperately fearful. They must be made aware of the diabolical evils of the present system and they must be called to repentance but they must also be given something to hope for. At the present they have false hopes. They hope to maintain the status quo and their special privileges with perhaps some adjustments and they fear any real alternative. But there is much more than that to hope for and nothing to fear. Can the Christian message of hope not help them in this matter?

There is hope. There is hope for all of us. But the road to that hope is going to be very hard and very painful. The conflict and the struggle will have to intensify in the months and years ahead because there is no other way to remove the injustice and oppression. But God is with us. We can only learn to become instruments of *his* peace even unto death. We must participate in the cross of Christ if we are to have the hope of participating in his resurrection.

Thankfulness for hopes fulfilled A Prayer from Crossroads
celebrating a reprieve 29 July 1979

Crossroads, the squatter community near Cape Town, was, until recently, under constant threat of demolition and removal.

We thank you, O God
You have answered us.
You have saved us together with our children
here in the place where you put us in your loving will.

We praise you, we sing of you, because you watch over this piece of land which is Crossroads.

You, O God, are to be praised
because you never let us fall into the hands of those
who would tear us apart.

O God, may you help us and our children in all our needs
just as you did the Israelites in the desert.

Our eyes have seen the evil which reigns over this land of
    ours — South Africa.
We have seen, O Lord, those who call themselves
    Christians, but who instead are used by Satan.
Enter their hearts and reveal to them the coming judgment.

Lord God of hosts, when we have you, we have all things.
When our enemies are upon us, we do not fear,
    because you said
that all who trust in you will not be disappointed.
We too, O Lord, have hope that you are present and supply
    our need.

You once spoke in the wilderness and stilled the
    dangerous snakes.
You have spoken your word even in this wilderness at
    Crossroads.
When enemies rose up against us, their strength failed.
Even death did not defeat us.
Just as David says: the Lord is my shepherd.
Our help is in the name of the Lord. Amen

Psalm 124

Setting by Bro. Clement Sithole OSB

Response: Our help is in the name of the Lord, in the name of the Lord.

If the Lord was not with us, let Israel now say
If the Lord was not with us, when the peoples attacked us
We would have been crushed to pieces. *(Response)*

In the Strength of God

The Christian life can only be lived in the strength of God. Christians, aware of the magnitude of their task, the weakness of their will, and the paucity of their own resources, depend upon the power of the Spirit. Waiting on God does not mean withdrawal from responsibility but a sensitivity and openness to God's will and purpose, and a reliance on God's strength.

Waiting for God

Isaiah 40:28-31 (RSV)

Have you not known? Have you not heard?
The Lord is the everlasting God,
the Creator of the ends of the earth.
He does not faint or grow weary,
his understanding is unsearchable.
He gives power to the faint,
and to him who has no might he increases strength.
Even youths shall faint and be weary,
and young men shall fall exhausted;
but they who wait for the Lord shall renew
their strength,
they shall mount up with wings like eagles,
they shall run and not be weary,
they shall walk and not faint.

Isaiah 64:1-5 (RSV)

O that thou wouldest rend the heavens
and come down,

that the mountains might quake at thy presence —
as when fire kindles brushwood
and the fire causes water to boil —
to make thy name known to thy adversaries,
and that the nations might tremble at thy presence!
When thou didst terrible things
which we looked not for,
thou camest down, the mountains quaked at thy presence.
From of old no one has heard
or perceived by the ear,
no eye has seen a God besides thee,
who works for those who wait for him.

Waiting and working

Andrew Murray[45]

The following extract is from the writings of Andrew Murray jnr. Undoubtedly the most eminent Dutch Reformed Church pastor and leader during the latter half of the nineteenth century, Murray's writings on Christian devotion and holiness gained worldwide recognition. Although deeply concerned about the welfare of the underprivileged and poor, Murray was a man of his times and party to the decision which led to the segregation of the Dutch Reformed Church.

Here we have two texts (Isaiah 40:31; 64:4) in which the connection between waiting and working is made clear. In the first we see that waiting brings the needed strength for working — that it fits for joyful and unwearied work. Waiting on God has its value in this: it makes us strong in work for God. The second reveals the secret of this strength. 'God works for those who wait for him.' The waiting on God secures the working of God for us and in us, out of which our work must spring. The two passages teach a great lesson, that as waiting on God lies at the root of all true working for God, so working for God must be the fruit of all true waiting on him. Our great need is to hold the two sides of the truth in perfect conjunction and harmony.

There are some who say they wait upon God, but who do not work for him. For this there may be various reasons.

[45] Andrew Murray, *The Best of Andrew Murray*, Baker, Grand Rapids, 1978, pp.207f.

Here is one who confounds true waiting on God (in living, direct intercourse with him as the Living One), and the devotion to him of the energy of the whole being, with the slothful, helpless waiting that excuses itself from all work until God, by some special impulse, has made work easy. Here is another who waits on God more truly, regarding it as one of the highest exercises of the Christian life, and yet has never understood that at the root of all true waiting there must lie the surrender and the readiness to be wholly fitted for God's use in the service of men. And here is still another who is ready to work as well as wait, but is looking for some great inflow of the Spirit's power to enable him to do mighty works, while he forgets that as a believer he already has the Spirit of Christ dwelling in him, that more grace is given only to those who are faithful in the little, and that it is only in working that we can be taught by the Spirit how to do the greater works. All such, and all Christians, need to learn that waiting has working for its object, that it is only in working that waiting can attain its full perfection and blessedness. It is as we elevate working for God to its true place, as the highest exercise of spiritual privilege and power, that the absolute need and the divine blessing of waiting on God can be fully known.

On the other hand, there are some, there are many, who work for God, but know little of what it is to wait on him. They have been led to take up Christian work, under the impulse of natural or religious feeling, at the bidding of a pastor or a society, with but very little sense of what a holy thing it is to work for God. They do not know that *God's work can be done only in God's strength, by God himself working in us.* They have never learned that, just as the Son of God could do nothing of himself, but that the Father in him did the work, as he lived in continual dependence before him, so, and much more, the believer can do nothing but as God works in him. They do not understand that his power can rest on us only as in utter weakness we depend upon him. And so they have no conception of a continual waiting on God as being one of the first and essential conditions of successful work. And Christ's church and the world are suffer-

In the strength of God

ing today, oh, so terribly, not only because so many of its members are not working for God, but because so much working for God is done without waiting on God.

A spirituality for today?

Leslie Stradling[46]

Christian spirituality is rooted in the incarnation and so considerations of social and cultural factors must come into it. Failure to understand this is not confined to any particular shade of churchmanship nor is there anything new or indeed South African about it. There are John Milton's famous words: 'I cannot praise a fugitive and cloistered virtue, unexercised and unbreathed, that never sallies out and sees her adversary but slinks out of the race where the immortal garland is to be won, not without dust and heat.' John Milton was a political Christian who was warning us against a spirituality that does not want to get its feet wet or its hands dirty.

But it is possible to go to the other extreme and find our spirituality solely in the realm of social and political action. The principal danger here is that we can easily separate ourselves from our spiritual roots and come to think that all that matters is what we *do*. In so much activity it is possible to lose all thought of God, and then we find ourselves more and more trying to do what we have to do in our own strength and not his.

Basically, spirituality does not change but new emphases and new expressions are needed in every generation. Old ways of prayer don't work for many people today, but the yearning is there. In today's South Africa we are at the intersection of many cultures. If we are to know God and live in a significant relationship with him we have to know ourselves, and that means knowing ourselves as South Africans. We have to be in South Africa and yet not of it, to be John as well as Peter, Mary as well as Martha, not only to

---

[46] Leslie Stradling, *A Bishop at Prayer*, SPCK, London, 1971, p.28f. Leslie Stradling was Anglican Bishop of Johannesburg.

pray for rain but to construct dams; and to hold prayer and action, truth and love, in creative tension.

A spirituality for us today will have a place for prophecy, with something to say, pray and do about squatters, the African National Congress and Black Sash.[47] It will include our outlook on sport, race, capitalism and socialism. It will be a spirituality in which prayer has a great place; it will involve the overcoming of personal sins and the cultivation of virtues; it will have a serious concern for justice, peace and reconciliation, for the oppressed, the victimised and the dehumanised. In the words of Dag Hammarskjold, 'in our age the road to holiness passes through the world of action'.

It is not uncommon to talk to God

Dennis Brutus[48]

A poem written from prison on Robben Island

Particularly in a single cell,
but even in the sections
the religious sense asserts itself;

perhaps a childhood habit of nightly prayers
the accessibility of Bibles,
or awareness of the proximity of death:

and, of course, it is a currency —
pietistic expressions can purchase favours
and it is a way of suggesting reformation
(which can procure promotion);

and the resort of the weak
is to invoke divine revenge
against a rampaging injustice;

but in the grey silence of the empty afternoons
it is not uncommon
to find oneself talking to God.

[47] The Black Sash is an organisation comprised of white women who since the 1950's have actively protested against apartheid legislation and its implementation.
[48] Dennis Brutus, *Letters to Martha and Other Poems from a South African Prison*, Heinneman, London, 1968, p.9.

Lord, teach us to pray

Tune: Missa Zimb.

Response: Our Father, who art in heaven, may your n.
be glorified.

Verses

Our Father — who art in heaven — hallowed be — thy n.

Thy kingdom come — thy will be done — on earth — as it
heaven

Give us this day — our daily bread — give us this day
our daily bread

And forgive us — forgive our sins — as we forgive — th
who sin against us

And lead us not — into temptation — but deliver us —
from evil

For the kingdom — and the power — and the glory — ar
thine

Now and forever — now and forever — Amen, amen —
amen, amen, Amen.

from the Nde

The Reality of Reconciliation

The Christian life is lived on the basis that God has reconciled the world to himself in Jesus Christ. The reconciling death of Christ on the cross is an event which has taken place in history, and it provides the basis for the reconciliation of warring factions within the human family.

Reconciliation through the cross   Ephesians 2:11-22 (NIV)

Therefore, remember that formerly you who are Gentiles by birth and called 'uncircumcised' by those who call themselves 'the circumcision' (that done in the body by the hands of men) — remember that at that time you were separate from Christ, excluded from citizenship in Israel and foreigners to the covenants of the promise, without hope and without God in the world. But now in Christ Jesus you who once were far away have been brought near through the blood of Christ.

For he himself is our peace, who has made the two one and has destroyed the barrier, the dividing wall of hostility, by abolishing in his flesh the law with its commandments and regulations. His purpose was to create in himself one new man out of the two, thus making peace, and in this one body to reconcile both of them to God through the Cross, by which he put to death their hostility. He came and preached peace to you who were far away and peace to those who were near. For through him we both have access to the Father by one Spirit.

Reconciliation and identification   C.F. Beyers Naude[49]

Dr. C.F. Beyers Naude, a former Moderator of the Transvaal Synod of the Dutch Reformed Church, was the Director of the Christian Institute of Southern Africa from its formation in 1963 until its banning by the government in 1977. In 1973 Beyers Naude and other members of the Christian Institute refused to give evidence to a government Commission of Inquiry into its activities on the grounds that the Commission was not judicial and public. This refusal was a legal offence and led to the trial of Beyers Naude in the Pretoria Magistrate's Court in November 1977. In the following extract Dr. Naude is being cross-examined by his advocate, Mr. Kriegler SC.

Q: Now, Mr. Naude, that line of thought, that point of view or opinion of yours in connexion with polarisation and black consciousness, how does it stand in contrast to or in line with the resolutions of Cottesloe, Lunteren and Sydney?[50]

A: You mean from my point of view, how I . . .?

Q: Yes.

A: I see this as the logical and obvious conclusion of the conviction which has been reflected from the days of Cottesloe, Lunteren and Sydney.

Q: And much more important, Mr. Naude, where does your point of view stand in relation to scripture?

A: I believe that this point of view interprets to the best of my knowledge the truth of the gospel as it was given to me by Jesus Christ.

Q: Can you for a moment explain the concept, the theological concept, 'reconciliation'?

A: Your Worship, the New Testament brings us the great and wonderful truth in the first place that God in Jesus Christ reconciled man in his lost and fallen state with God. Paul is one of the greatest exponents of this Christian

---

[49] *The Trial of Beyers Naude: Christian Witness and the rule of law,* edited by the International Commission of Jurists, Geneva. Search Press, London, 1975, p.91f.

[50] *Cottesloe* refers to the Cottesloe Consultation held in Johannesburg by the South African member churches of the World Council of Churches in 1960 in response to Sharpeville; *Lunteren* and *Sydney* refer to two synods of the Reformed Ecumenical Synod held in 1968 and 1972 respectively. At all three events there were official delegations of the Dutch Reformed Church.

truth in his letters to the congregation at Corinth. It follows from this as a matter of course that because God worked this reconciliation in Christ it is part, indissolubly and unreservedly and eternally, it is part of the life and witness of the Christian, that he must reconcile himself with his neighbour and he should do all in his power to reconcile his neighbour with himself and his neighbour with another, who are in conflict, in opposition and alienation and in bitterness against each other. This is the heart of the gospel.

Q: Where does this stand in relation to the second great commandment?

A: It is a natural result of it, where Christ said to us that the commandment to love God is summarised in the first and the great commandment of love to God and the second that you should love your neighbour as yourself, and these two commandments are the law and the prophets.

Q: And what relation is there between the concept 'reconciliation' and the theological concept of 'identification'?

A: No reconciliation is possible without justice, and whoever works for reconciliation must first determine the causes of injustice in the hearts and lives of those, of either the persons or groups, who feel themselves aggrieved. In order to determine the causes of the injustice a person must not only have the outward individual facts of the matter, but as a Christian you are called to identify yourself in heart and soul, to live in, to think in, and to feel in the heart, in the consciousness, the feelings of the person or the persons who feel themselves aggrieved. This is the grace that the new birth in Jesus Christ gives a person, every person who wishes to receive it.

Reconciliation and liberation   T.A. Mofokeng[51]

In the Bible the objective reality of reconciliation is con-

[51] An edited extract from an unpublished paper by the Dr. T.A. Mofokeng of the Dutch Reformed Church in Africa, given at a conference on 'The possibilities of reconciliation for Blacks and Whites in South Africa Today' organized by the Christian Academy of Southern Africa, October 1975.

nected with divine liberation. Human fellowship with God is made possible through his intervention in history, in our world, setting people free from economic, social and political bondage. When we look closer at the history of Israel as found in the Bible it becomes abundantly clear that there could have been no covenant at Sinai without the Exodus, no reconciliation without liberation. We also find a close relationship between reconciliation and liberation in the New Testament. Christ is the reconciler because he is first the liberator. He was baptised with sinners, walked and lived with the poor and oppressed — he was the oppressed one sent from God to give wholeness to broken lives.

Too many people believe, however, in the liberation of people as an act of God's intervention in history as though all of us should leave everything up to him. He does not need our agency. This cannot be the correct understanding of God's activity in the affairs of the world. It has a side that requires the active involvement of people as agents of reconciliation. God transforms people and makes them agents in his service of liberation of the poor and oppressed. When we read that 'Christ is our peace, who has made us both one and has broken down the dividing wall of hostility,' and we try to translate this into the language and circumstances of our time, we must see ourselves involved in active affirmation of this truth through our negation of anything that rejects its validity. 'There can be no reconciliation with God unless the hungry are fed, the sick are healed and justice is given to the poor' (James Cone).

I strongly believe in the existence of the possibility for reconciliation in our country. This may not become a reality in our time but certainly in that of our sons and daughters. But this cannot be realised without a price to be paid by white and black people who are committed Christians and firm believers in the equality of all people. There is no possibility of reconciliation between black and white people in this country until the oppressive structures and institutions, be they black or white, are transformed and put into service for the benefit of the underprivileged majority of this beautiful land.

Where the rainbow ends

Richard Rive[52]

Where the rainbow ends,
There's going to be a place brother,
Where the world can sing all sorts of songs,
And we're going to sing, together, brother,
You and I,
Though you're White and I'm not.
It's going to be a sad song, brother,
'Cause we don't know the tune,
And it's a difficult tune to learn,
But we can learn it, brother,
You and I,
There's no such tune as a Black tune,
There's no such tune as a White tune,
There's only music, brother,
And it's music, we're going to sing,
Where the rainbow ends.

Prayer for racial harmony[53]

O Lord Jesus Christ, you were sent of our Father
to set all captives free,
Send down upon us, your frail servants and brothers,
your promised Holy Spirit,
that this land beloved of us and you,
may be redeemed from the sin of shameful division and
    discord.
Come deliver us
from the captivity of fear and greed that keeps us apart.
You who died for us while we were yet sinners,
lead us to die to our pride and selfish ambitions
and the easy complacency with injustice in our land,
to the lust for power and mastery over others.
Teach us Lord to acknowledge none but you as 'Master' and
    'Baas'.

[52] Richard Rive, 'Where the Rainbow Ends' in *The Return of the Aamasi Bird*, p.155. First published in *Drum*, May 1955.
[53] An edited version of a prayer published in *Pro Veritate*, March 1973. Author and source unknown.

Lord, save us from servility and the agony of despair
at the relentless cruelty of our circumstance,
from our vicious treatment of one another,
and the anguish of bitterness, resentment and hatred.
Lord, your prophet long ago forsaw the day
when the lion and the wolf shall lie down with the lamb:
give now to us the day when black and white
shall stand side by side and
together fall down at your feet.
In you only Christ Jesus, by the power of your Spirit
can we love our God and one another as you have loved us,
that joy, peace and harmony may rule our land. Amen.

Christ enough

John B. Gardener

The words of this hymn were written by a school teacher, John Gardener, for a Methodist city mission in Cape Town and Pretoria in 1963. It has been widely used since then at church conferences, in youth groups, and more generally. The origin of the tune is not clear, but it was probably a missionary adaptation of an African original. It appears in the 1889 edition of the Xhosa Wesleyan Hymn Book as the second tune for the hymn 'Nkosi yam' ('My Lord') and is popularly known by that name. The hymn 'Love divine, all loves excelling' is often sung to 'Nkosi yam'.

Who will save our land and people
Who can rescue us from wrong?
We are lost, faint, false and foolish
We have slighted God too long.
Save the people, Lord our Saviour

Guide us home from country far;
Holy Fire, consume our rancours
Thy Kingdom come in Africa.

Make our land as clean and wholesome
As the white of sea-washed sands;
Stretch our vision vast and boundless
As our brown-spread dusty lands
Make our people strong and steadfast
As the hills that claw our sky;
Hear our prayer for land and people
God Bless Africa we cry.

We believe God is our Saviour
Christ enough to heal our land
He will use the Church, his servants
We on earth his out-stretched hand
May his church in loving service
Show to all whose path is rough
Give a clear, united witness
And proclaim 'Christ is enough'.

Christ enough to break all barriers
Christ enough in peace, in strife
Christ enough to build our nation
Christ enough for death, for life
Christ enough for old and lonely
Christ enough for those who fall
Christ enough to save the sin-sick
Christ enough for one, for all.

The Conversion of the Church

The Christian life is lived within the community of the church of J
Christ. Christianity while personal is never individualistic; Chris
are 'members one of another' within the 'body of Christ'. The ch
is at the same time a community of sinners and saints. Becau
members are human the church is sinful and in continual nee
renewal and reformation so that it can bear a faithful witness t
gospel.

Do not be conformed   Romans 12:1-2 (

Therefore, I urge you, brothers, in view of God's merc
offer your bodies as living sacrifices, holy and pleasin
God — which is your spiritual worship. Do not conform
longer to the pattern of this world, but be transformed b
renewing of your mind. Then you will be able to test
approve what God's will is — his good, pleasing and pe
will.

The Belhar Confession of Faith

In 1982 the Dutch Reformed Mission Church adopted a new
Confession of Faith at its Synod meeting at Belhar, Cape Town.
Confession was a positive response to and affirmation of the de
tion that Apartheid is a Heresy.[54]

[54] This extract from the Belhar Confession is taken from G.D. Cloete and D.J. S
Moment of Truth: the Confession of the Dutch Reformed Mission Church 1982, Eerd
Grand Rapids, 1984, pp.2f.

We believe that God has entrusted to his Church the message of reconciliation in and through Jesus Christ; that the Church is called to be the salt of the earth and the light of the world; that the church is called blessed because it is a peacemaker; that the church is witness both by word and deed to the new heaven and the new earth in which righteousness dwells;

that God by giving his lifegiving Word and Spirit has conquered the powers of sin and death, and therefore also of irreconciliation and hatred, bitterness and enmity; that God by his lifegiving Word and Spirit will enable his people to live in a new obedience which can open new possibilities for society and the world;

that the credibility of this message is seriously affected and its beneficial work obstructed when it is proclaimed in a land which professes to be Christian, but in which the enforced separation of people on a racial basis promotes and perpetuates alienation, hatred, and enmity;

that any teaching which attempts to legitimate such forced separation by appeal to the gospel and is not prepared to venture on the road of obedience and reconciliation, but rather, out of prejudice, fear, selfishness, and unbelief, denies in advance the reconciling power of the gospel, must be considered ideology and false doctrine.

The Alternative Community   David Bosch[55]

I am increasingly convinced that the situation in our country, among us Christians, will become worse until we realise that we have to begin with ourselves. What is necessary is that we all move from where we are and converge at another point, even the foot of the cross. This is not going to be easy. We think that a normal amount of goodwill and ordinary human decency will carry us through. We believe that if all can see things as we do, our problems will be solved soon. We are convinced that we ourselves have come a long way.

[55] Adapted and edited from *Be Transformed*, 2/2. A Dutch Reformed theologian, Dr. David Bosch is Professor of Missiology at the University of South Africa.

All this is self-deception. Applying our goodwill and decency to the South African society is like applying sticking-plaster to a running sore.

The real stumbling-block often happens to be the church herself — the very church whose raison d'etre is precisely to be a pointer to Christ and to attract others to him. The church too often fulfils the role of a social agency for the relief of painful disappointments; she is the place where uncomprehended fears are suppressed, where uncomfortable memories and awkward expectations are being covered up. The church has become the cosy ghetto of kindred souls, the cave into which we flee when the day-to-day problems are too much for us. The church has to provide the snug atmosphere of a comfortable living room with a fire glowing in the hearth, quiet music in the background and a glass of wine in the hand. In such a church people think in the categories of prosperity and success rather than the cross. The Good News then becomes what people wish to hear because it soothes them. No, more than that: it drugs them, it becomes the 'opiate of the people'. If we define the church — however subconsciously — in these categories, it means that we want to see results, that we want to report progress, that we judge the church according to the dividends she produces. She then adapts to her environment.

Instead of turning the world upside down, we keep it neatly in position so that nobody is caught off-balance. Instead of causing people to stare in amazement at the newness and sparkle of our community life, we irritate those outside or make them yawn because we bore them. Instead of drawing people to us, we repel them. This is the deepest reason why we have to stage evangelism campaigns and other special programmes in order to boost our membership and make our tarnished image a bit more respectable. But precisely these evangelistic campaigns often become utterly self-defeating because of the shallowness of the life of the church into which we receive new converts. We often resemble a farmer who carries sheaves into his burning barn.

We have called her the 'alternative community', however.

And the whole thrust of that word is that there can be only *one* alternative, one *alter*. What Jesus offers is the only alternative to all the other options. In this alternative community we are not asked about the extent of our successes but about the depth of our obedience. We have been so inveigled by the success ethic, says Desmond Tutu, we forget that, in many ways, we were *meant* to be a failing community.

These are the strange paradoxes of the alternative community: it is only when we leave self behind that we find ourselves; it is only when we serve that we are free; it is only when we are prepared to suffer that we experience true joy; it is only when we die that we live. Is not this what Paul also said? '. . . we are imposters who speak the truth, the unknown men whom all men know: dying we still live on; disciplined by suffering, we are not done to death: in sorrows we have always cause for joy; poor ourselves, we bring wealth to many; penniless, we own the world' (2 Corinthians 6:8-10   NEB).

Just a passerby

Oswald Joseph Mtshali[56]

I saw them clobber him with kieries,
I heard him scream with pain
like a victim of slaughter;
I smelt fresh blood gush
from his nostrils,
and flow on the street.

I walked into the church,
and knelt in the pew,
'Lord! I love you,
I also love my neighbour. Amen'

I came out
my heart as light as an angel's kiss
on the cheek of a saintly soul.

[56] Oswald Joseph Mtshali, *Sounds of a Cowhide Drum*, Renoster, Johannesburg, 1971, p.56.

Back home I strutted
past a crowd of onlookers.
Then she came in —
my woman neighbour:
'Have you heard? They've killed your brother.'
'Oh! No! I heard nothing. I've been to church.'

Critics of the church

Alan Pa

It is one of the good signs of our times that there is such
criticism within the church. This self-criticism is pract
by both clergy and laity. It is very different from the critic
of those who are outside the church, and would not part
larly want the church to succeed in practising wha
preaches. Nor is it the same as the criticism of those whc
members of the church, who perpetually criticise the chu
and especially the clergy because it is their scapegoat
their own failures. I mean the criticism of those who are f
in the church, who are distressed by the way it often ada
itself to the 'pattern of this present world,' who want to s
a witness for Christ in the world. The trouble with witn
ing for Christ in the world is that it is at times almost imp
ible not to antagonise the rich, the well-established,
ruling classes, and important people within the chu
itself.

Rend your hearts

Joel 2:12-17 (

'Even now,' declares the Lord,
'return to me with all your heart,
with fasting and weeping and mourning.'

Rend your heart
and not your garments.
Return to the Lord your God,
for he is gracious and compassionate,
slow to anger and abounding in love,

---

[57] Alan Paton, *Instrument of Thy Peace, op. cit.,* p.79.

and he relents from sending calamity.
Who knows but that he may turn
and have pity
and leave behind a blessing —
grain offerings and drink offerings
for the Lord your God.

Blow the trumpet in Zion,
declare a holy fast,
call a sacred assembly.
Gather the people,
consecrate the assembly;
bring together the elders,
gather the children,
those nursing at the breast.
Let the bridegroom leave his room
and the bride her chamber.
Let the priests, who minister,
weep between the temple porch
and the altar.
Let them say, 'Spare your people,
O Lord.
Do not make your inheritance an
object of scorn,
a byword among the nations.
Why should they say among the people,
"where is your God?"'

Renew your church, Lord

Renew your church, Lord,
your people in this land.
Save us from cheap words
and self-deception in your service.

In the power of your Spirit
transform us,
and shape us
by your cross.

Sharing a Common Life

The Christian life lived in common with others is a life of commitment to one another in Christ in the service of the world. It is the joy of this common life in Christ that Christians wish to share with others.

A testimony to the life we share
1 John 1:1-4 (NEB)

It was there from the beginning; we have heard it; we have seen it with our own eyes; we have looked upon it, and felt it with our own hands; and it is of this we tell. Our theme is the word of life. This life was made visible; we have seen it and bear our testimony; we here declare to you the eternal life which dwelt with the Father and was made visible to us. What we have seen and heard we declare to you, so that you and we together may share in a common life, that life which we share with the Father and his Son Jesus Christ. And we write this in order that the joy of us all may be complete.

The ultimate purpose of human life   Alphaeus Zulu[58]

John used these words to explain the purpose of his writing. According to him the ultimate purpose of human life is that men and women 'may have a common life' in the world. Our instincts lead us to agree with John. This is precisely the goal of all organisations. Communities, nations, races, nationalisms, fascisms, communisms, tribes, families, couples, siblings — all desire, seek, struggle, hate and even kill, in the desperate effort to find, maintain and expand a common life. There is restless agitation in every human breast and in every generation until this goal is reached. Let us then contemplate the gratitude and the joy that filled John's heart when he wrote these words. He was honest with himself and with his people. He acknowledged his personal empty restlessness and that of his group until he found satisfaction and meaning in Jesus Christ.

According to John, God came in the flesh in order that we might share a common life with him. However, openness is required of those who would experience the joy of this privilege. John and a few others were always on the alert, listening, watching, following, and ready to receive. But as in his day, the tragedy of the world is that it tends to choose 'darkness rather than the light'. It persists in seeking a common life outside Jesus Christ where it shall never be found. God the Father of Jesus Christ alone is the source of the common life that endures.

John asks us to acknowledge our failure to find community and fellowship where we have preferred to look for it. He tells us of the love of God expressed for us in Jesus, through whom we may be transformed and so share a common life with the Father and one another. But like John, we must be open to that love and to Jesus Christ if we are going to share in this common life, and share it with others.

---

[58] Alphaeus Zulu, 'A Christmas Meditation', *Journal of Theology for Southern Africa*, no. 9, December 1974, p.7f. Alphaeus Zulu, former Anglican Bishop of Zululand, was also a President of the World Council of Churches.

Solidarity in prayer

Desmond T▮

On December 2, 1984, Bishop Desmond Tutu preached in W▮
ington Cathedral at a service of Thanksgiving on his being awar▮
the Nobel Peace Prize. The following is an extract from his serm▮

This service is in thanksgiving to God. I want to add my o▮
thanks to you. We Christians believe that in becomin▮
Christian you become a member of the body of Christ ▮
part of a worldwide fellowship. You have brothers ▮
sisters scattered over the face of the earth.

We know, too, that we are by our humanity member▮
the human family and thereby sisters and brothers in m▮
lands. And we know in our experience what it has me▮
to be upheld by the love and prayers and the concer▮
so many around the world. It has been almost a phys▮
sensation, this being borne up by those servant prayer▮

Christians

James Matthe▮

Christians
that is what they term themselves.
Sundays garbed in black and grey
they fill their churches' pews
faces turned towards the heavens
praying their God for their accorded task
rulers of the land; the chosen ones

Christians
their serfs seated in another church
told to serve without qualm
their master's demand

Christians
with pious right they sit and plot
dividing God's beaches and his land
ensuring that the fairest go to them

---

[59] Desmond Tutu, 'On Behalf of Millions', published in *Sojourners*, February
pp.24f.
[60] James Matthews, 'Christians', in Basil Moore (ed.), *The Challenge of Black Theol▮
South Africa*, John Knox, Atlanta, 1973, p.64.

the little that is left
shared out among the many
who have no say and forced to
accept the desperation of their plight

Christians
unconcerned about those who sit and starve
whose crops, like themselves, die in arid soil
and others removed from the land they love

Christians
what welcome would they give God's son
confronted with the classification board
and identification card stating race
then consigned to his proper place
would be banned for his message
that love has no colour connotation
that the brotherhood of man is all-embracing?

Christians
who deport priests for performing God's work
will not hesitate to proclaim an order
declaring the son of God an agitator.

The black dilemma
Alphaeus Zulu[61]

Some black people consider themselves resolutely committed to fellowship among men regardless of colour and to
work for reconciliation where animosities exist. But fellowship and reconciliation, however, are the fruit of collaboration between parties. Of recent years, the 'other form of
separation', in education, in employment and in social
relations, has succeeded so well that a big gap has grown
between white and black. Without mutual and effective
communication how do people become friends, and if there
may be no friendships how do black and white come to trust
one another?

[61] Alphaeus Zulu, *The Dilemma of the Black South African*, T.B. Davie Lecture, University of Cape Town, 1972.

What the Christian gospel says

The Message to the People of South Africa[62]

The Message to the People of South Africa was prepared by a Theological Commission of the South African Council of Churches and adopted by the SACC in 1968. It was the first major ecumenical theological statement adopted by SACC member churches in which apartheid is explicitly rejected as a false gospel.

The Gospel of Jesus Christ
 is the good news that in Christ God has broken down the walls of division between God and man, and therefore also between man and man.

The Gospel of Jesus Christ
 declares that Christ is the truth who sets men free from all false hopes of grasping freedom for themselves, and that Christ liberates them from a pursuit of false securities.

The Gospel of Jesus Christ
 declares that, in the crucifixion of Jesus, sin has been forgiven, and that God has met and mastered the forces that threaten to isolate man and destroy him.

The Gospel of Jesus Christ
 declares that, in the resurrection of Jesus, God showed himself as the conqueror and destroyer of the most potent of all forms of separation, namely death, and he proved the power of his love to overthrow the evil powers of fear, envy and pride which cause hostility between men.

The Gospel of Jesus Christ
 declares that, by this work of Christ, men are being reconciled to God and to each other, and that excluding barriers of ancestry, race, nationality, language and culture, have no rightful place in the inclusive brotherhood of Christian disciples.

The Gospel of Jesus Christ
 declares that God is the master of this world, that his is the mind and purpose that shapes history, and that it is to him alone, and not to any subsection of humanity, that we owe our primary obedience and commitment.

---

[62] 'The Message to the People of South Africa' is published in John W. de Gruchy and Charles Villa-Vicencio, *Apartheid is a Heresy*, Eerdmans, Grand Rapids, 1983, p.154.

The Gospel of Jesus Christ
declares that we live in the expectation of a new heaven
and a new earth in which righteousness dwells; that the
Kingdom of God is present already in Christ and through
the Holy Spirit; and that it therefore now demands our
obedience to his commandments and our faith in his
promises.

Prayer at the end of a conference   Klaus Nurnberger

*The following prayer was offered extemporaneously at the end of a
conference held in 1985 at which an attempt was made to resolve
theological and other conflicts within some churches in South Africa.*

Dear Lord, we thank you for the time we had together
that after initial disappointments, suspicions and hurts
we began to find each other;
that the silence of those who decided not to join us
began to communicate;
that after initial hopelessness and gloom
we began to regain some hope for the future of our country.

We pray for those we have left behind in our thinking,
those who would be horrified by what has been said
    amongst us,
who would consider us traitors.

We pray for those who are ahead of us,
who would consider our little battles as irrelevant for their
    struggle,
whose patience with our hesitations has run out.

We pray for our land,
which is your land;
we pray for ourselves, wanting to be your servants.
Show us the way you want us to go,
the role you wish us to play in your redemptive work,
and the courage to place that above all else.   Amen.

Christian Freedom

The Christian life is one of freedom. Freedom is not licence to do what we like. Freedom is a gift which enables us to be responsible to God and towards others. Christian freedom is that liberty which, as Martin Luther said, makes us slaves of none yet servants of all.

Freedom in Christ

Galatians 5:1-6, 13-14 (N

It is for freedom that Christ has set us free. Stand firm, then and do not let yourselves be burdened by the yoke of slavery. Mark my words! I, Paul, tell you that if you let yourselves circumcised, Christ will be of no value to you at all. I declare to every man who lets himself be circumcised that he is obligated to obey the whole law. You who are trying to be justified by law have been alienated from Christ; you have fallen away from grace. But by faith we eagerly await through the Spirit the righteousness for which we hope. For in Christ Jesus neither circumcision nor uncircumcision has any value. The only thing that counts is faith expressing itself through love. You my brothers, were called to be free. But not use your freedom to indulge the sinful nature; rather serve one another in love. The entire law is summed up in a single command: 'Love your neighbour as yourself.'

188

Freedom to be for others
Theodore Simpson[63]

I do not wish to deny, indeed I wish to affirm, that something objectively happened on the cross. What happened was that God made a total commitment of himself to the despair, suffering, defeat and death which are characteristic of our alienated condition. In so doing he revealed himself definitely and once-for-all as a God of suffering love who claims the lost, the unworthy, the rejected and the self-rejecting as his own. This is a *decisive* act of liberation just because it involves a total immersion in the human condition, even to the point of death. It is an act of acceptance which is an irreplaceable and incontrovertible sign to us that God suffers with us and accepts us in our sin and suffering. Thus at one stroke it undercuts the destructive fears, the guilt and anxiety which possesses and enslaves us, and inaugurates a new and healing relationship between God and those who have experienced the power of the good news of the death and resurrection of the Lord.

At the same time, I do not wish to deny, but rather to affirm, that we need to be transformed subjectively; that we are possessed by destructive powers which enslave us. We can now see more clearly in the light of some modern psychology how it is possible for individuals and even whole societies to be gripped by obsessive fears which seem to be stronger than they are. We are thus in a better position to understand why individuals fall prey to irrational and self-destructive behaviour, and why even whole societies may fall under bondage to destructive forces like racism and economic exploitation. What is more, we can now see that the root of these problems is to be found in individual and collective self-hatred and self-distrust, and that the remedy for them lies in the divine truth which has the power to set us free.

Obviously there is much more that might be said about this, and I would not wish to be misunderstood as implying, for example, that structural and institutionalised racism and

[63] An edited extract from Theodore Simpson, 'A Very Present Help', *Journal of Theology for Southern Africa*, no. 21. Dr. Simpson was formerly Principal of St. Peter's Anglican College at the Federal Theological Seminary.

exploitation can be destroyed without a change in the structures which make people what they are. But the revelation of God in Jesus Christ is a saving revelation because it delivers us from the inhibiting restrictions of fear and guilt and sets us free for a new kind of relationship with God and with our neighbour.

Free to be human

Desmond Tutu[64]

We are made for fellowship, for community, most wonderfully with our creator. Anything less than God cannot satisfy our hunger for God. Equally we are made for fellowship with others, and any ordering of society which puts up barriers between persons is blasphemous because it denies what God has said about human beings 'made in the image of God'. One section of the community cannot truly be free while another is denied a share in that freedom. We are involved in the black liberation struggle because we are also deeply concerned for white liberation.

Whites will never be really free until blacks are wholly free. Whites invest enormous resources in trying to gain a fragile security and peace, resources which should have been used more creatively elsewhere. Whites must suffer too, because they are bedevilled by anxiety and fear. God wants to set them free, to set us all free *from* all that dehumanises us, to set us free *for* our service of one another in a more just and open society. It will be a society where true peace, justice and righteousness will prevail, where we will have real reconciliation because we will be people whose God-given dignity is respected, where we will be free to carry out the obligations and responsibilities of being human.

A Litany of Confession

Cathedral Church of St George, Cape Town[65]

Lord, we confess our day to day failure to be human
Lord, we confess to you

---

[64] Extracts from Desmond Tutu, 'God-given Dignity and the Quest for Liberation in the Light of the South African Dilemma', in *Liberation*, SACC, Johannesburg, 1976, pp.56f.
[65] Vigil of Prayer for Detainees, 25 Agust 1975.

Lord, we confess that we often fail to love with all we have and are, often because we do not fully understand what loving means, often because we are afraid of risking ourselves.

Lord, we confess to you

Lord, we cut ourselves off from each other and we erect barriers of division.

Lord, we confess to you

Lord, we confess that by silence and ill-considered word

We have built up walls of prejudice

Lord, we confess that by selfishness and lack of sympathy

We have stifled generosity and left little time for others

Holy Spirit, speak to us. Help us to listen to your word of forgiveness, for we are very deaf. Come fill this moment and free us from our sin.

Some potent thrust to freedom

Dennis Brutus[66]

O let me soar on steadfast wing
that those who know me for a pitiable thing
may see me inerasably clear:

grant that their faith that I might hood
some potent thrust to freedom, humanhood
under drab fluff may still be justified.

Protect me from the slightest deviant swoop
to pretty bush or hedgerow lest I droop
ruffled or trifled, snared or power misspent.

Uphold — frustrate me if need be
so that I mould my energy
for that one swift inerrable soar

hurling myself swordbeaked to lunge
for lodgement in my life's sun-targe —
a land and people just and free.

---

[66] Originally entitled 'Prayer' this poem by Dennis Brutus was published in his anthology *Letters to Martha, op. cit.*, p.33.

24

Obedience
to God

The Christian life confesses that Jesus is Lord. This is a costly a
demanding confession of faith which inevitably brings Christians i
conflict with an unjust social order.

Blessed be the God who deals justice

Psalm 1

Praise the Lord, praise the Lord O my soul:
while I live I will praise the Lord;

While I have any being:
I will sing praises to my God.

Put not your trust in princes:
nor in the sons of men, who cannot save.

For when their breath goes from them,
   they return again to the earth:
and on that day all their thoughts perish.

Blessed is the man whose help is the God of Jacob:
whose hope is in the Lord his God,

The God who made heaven and earth:
the sea, and all that is in them,

Who keeps faith for ever:
who deals justice to those who are oppressed.

The Lord gives food to the hungry:
and sets the captives free.

The Lord gives sight to the blind:
the Lord lifts up those who are bowed down.

The Lord loves the righteous:
the Lord cares for the stranger in the land.

He upholds the widow and the fatherless:
as for the way of the wicked, he turns it upside down.

The Lord shall be king for ever:
your God, O Zion, shall reign through all generations.
Praise the Lord.

Obey God not man
Acts 5:25-32 (NIV)

Then someone came and said 'Look! The men you put in jail are standing in the temple courts teaching the people.' At that, the captain went with his officers and brought the apostles. They did not use force, because they feared the people would stone them. Having brought the apostles, they made them appear before the Sanhedrin to be questioned by the high priest. 'We gave you strict orders not to teach in this name,' he said. 'Yet you have filled Jerusalem with your teaching and are determined to make us guilty of this man's blood.' Peter and the other apostles replied: 'We must obey God rather than men! The God of our fathers raised Jesus from the dead — whom you killed by hanging him on a tree. God exalted him to his own right hand as Prince and Saviour that he might give repentance and forgiveness of sins to Israel. We are witnesses to these things, and so is the Holy Spirit, whom God has given to those who obey him.'

I am first and foremost a Christian
Debora Patta[67]

During 1983 sixteen University students belonging to the Students' Union for Christian Action used street theatre at various public venues to protest the constant harrassment of squatters at KTC, part of the Crossroads squatter community near Cape Town. All sixteen were arrested for illegal gathering and were eventually found guilty, fined R100 and given a suspended prison sentence of three months. In her final statement to the magistrate, one of the students said:

[67] Originally published in *Between the Lines*, the newspaper of the Students' Union for Christian Action, August 1984, p.8f.

Your worship, the court has chosen to find me guilty of wrongfully and unlawfully attending an illegal gathering and it is now my task to explain why I did what I did on August 13, 1983.

I am a Christian and increasingly over the years I have realised that as a Christian there are certain demands and expectations I must live up to. Isaiah declares:

> Stop doing wrong, learn to do right! Seek justice, encourage the oppressed. Defend the cause of the fatherless. Plead the cause of the widow (Isaiah 1:15).

Again in Isaiah we read:

> The Spirit of the Sovereign Lord is upon me because the Lord has anointed me to preach good news to the poor. He has sent me to bind up the broken-hearted, to proclaim freedom for the captives and release for the prisoners (Isaiah 61).

Finally Amos declares:

> Let justice roll on like a river, righteousness like a never-failing stream (Amos 5:24).

These three passages quoted here are but a few examples of the theme repeated over and again in the Bible — to seek justice and speak out against all that is unjust.

Last year the state took action against the KTC squatters who were either squatting illegally or legally. Those classified as illegals were men, women and children who faced continued harassment simply to stay together as families; who chose to squat illegally; to work in Cape Town rather than face starvation and certain death in the so-called 'homelands'. Those squatting legally continued to do so because they had no access to decent housing and living conditions. Yet the state pulled down the sparse temporary shelters of these illegals, tear-gassed them and erected barbed wire around the area. The government then proposed as a solution the removal of all black persons to Khayelitsha, about 50 kilometres from places of work and far away from transport services. These people were to be removed from poverty-stricken conditions to even worse ones. The illegals were to be shunted back to the bantustans.

As a Christian I must judge this situation in the light of scripture. I read that the Bible abhors the break up of families and any ideology that proclaims inequality for people created as equals in God's image.

> There is neither Jew nor Greek, slave nor free, male nor female, for you are all one in Christ Jesus (Galatians 3:28).

But apartheid is preached in South Africa where whites are regarded as superhuman and blacks as less than human. Furthermore the land is divided unequally to preserve this apartheid and its ethnic divisions. The figures are well-known: 17 per cent white population to 87 per cent of the land, and 83 per cent black population to 13 per cent of the land.

The Bible tells us that the land is God's and to be equally distributed. It is unacceptable to God to have a small group of people allotted to a large proportion of land. It is against God's will to move people off their land without their consent; to break up communities and families; to remove their ability to enjoy the fruits of the land. It is against God's will when power-bearers allocate land to members of the power-bearing group primarily with a view to organising that group's security and asserting their dominance over their fellow human-beings.

Yet removals, poor living conditions, apartheid, economic oppression all continue — as illustrated in the KTC harassments and proposed removals to Khayelitsha — enforced by a 'Christian' country and yet fundamentally against God's will. So in the face of such injustice, such suffering, how could I as a Christian claiming God as my only Sovereign remain silent?

On August 13, 1983 I participated in a play in Claremont illustrating the injustice of removals in South Africa and calling people to respond. Your worship, I went not to break any law but to do that which is right in the eyes of God — to protest against injustices at KTC and Khayelitsha and to encourage the public of Cape Town to respond in some way.

If any law prevented me from doing this, I must needs ha
disregarded it. Calvin the great Christian leader of
Reformed tradition once commented: 'We are subject
those who rule over us but subject only in the Lord. If th
command anything against God let us not pay the le
regard to it.'

As a Christian my ultimate allegiance is to God who c
me into radical obedience away from evil and injustice — a
in God my conscience transcends the authority of the sta
Ultimately this higher loyalty to God's kingdom relativi
all earthly loyalties: God's law can make human law irre
vant; God's power can make human power inconsequent

The state has the right to expect my cooperation in all la
and policies that are just but how can I retain my integrit
a Christian and cooperate with all those laws and poli
that are unjust ones? I cannot obey two Gods — that is
first holy commandment.

So I conclude, your worship, by saying I was motivate
participate in a campaign about KTC to help effect some j
tice. What I did was insignificant compared to the sufferi
of the KTC people but what I did was biblical and Christi
The court has found me guilty of attending an illegal gath
ing but even so I must say that I will continue to seek a
proclaim justice in our land even though it may enta
breaking of this law or any other such laws designed
maintain an unjust status quo. I am proud to be able to
that I am first and foremost in my life a Christian and v
always obey God before the state.

Forgive us our folly   Presbyterian Church of Southern A

The General Assembly of the Presbyterian Church of Southern A
in 1984 authorised and commended the use of the following pra

O Lord God, we come before you in humility recognis
that we have sinned against you by governing this land w
laws that oppress and cause much harm and suffering
people. We have actively followed a system based on neit
love nor justice. We have resorted to violence to maint

this system, and this in turn is leading to more violence. Forgive us our folly.

We pray that you will deliver us and bring change to our situation. If it is your will to remove from office those rulers who have misgoverned and oppressed and who have mis-used the authority with which they have been invested, we ask for courage to do our part in this and wisdom to choose leaders who will obey your will, enact just laws and eradic-ate the evils and divisions that we have allowed to have dominion over us.

This we ask in the name of Jesus Christ. Amen.

You gave us, Lord, by word and deed Denis Hurley[68]

You gave us, Lord, by word and deed
The way of love your Father willed
That those who go where'er you lead
May find in you a life fulfilled.

It was your joy to call them blest
Who poor in spirit choose to be,
And find themselves of earth possessed,
The gentle heirs of all they see.

And blessed too are those who mourn,
The merciful, the pure of heart,
And those by thirst and hunger torn
That justice hold its rightful part.

Your blessing, Lord, embraces too
All those who strive that peace may reign,
Who right uphold and justice do
And face withal contempt and pain.

We humbly ask your pardon, Lord;
The ones that hear are all too few.
So speak again your healing word,
Our sin forgive, our heart renew.

Tune, Rockingham

[68] A hymn specially composed for the ecumenical agency for social action, Diakonia, Durban, by Archbishop Hurley. Published in *Diakonia News*, March 1979, p.10.

25

Witness
to Peace

*The Christian life is a sharing of the peace of Christ with our friends,
neighbours and enemies. Biblical peace, or shalom, is not cheap or
easy, it is the costly peace which required the death of Christ on the
cross. Christians witness to the 'peace of God which is beyond understanding'.*

Swords into ploughshares   Micah 4:2-5 (NIV)

Many nations will come and say,

'Come, let us go up to the
mountain of the Lord,
to the house of the God of Jacob.
He will teach us his ways,
so that we may walk in his paths.'

The law will go out from Zion,
the word of the Lord from Jerusalem.
He will judge between many peoples
and will settle disputes for strong nations far and wide.

They will beat their swords into ploughshares
and their spears into pruning hooks.
Nation will not take up sword against nation,
nor will they train for war anymore.
Everyman will sit under his own vine
and under his own fig tree,

and no one will make them afraid,
for the Lord Almighty has spoken.

All nations may walk
in the name of their gods;
we will walk in the name of the Lord
our God for ever and ever.

Peace testimony

Richard Steele

Richard Steele was one of the first religious conscientious objectors in South Africa. At the time of his year long imprisonment in Military Detention he was a member of the Baptist Church. Because he and his cousin, Peter Moll, another Baptist serving a prison sentence for conscientious objection at the same time, refused to wear army prison uniform as it implied compromise of principle, they spent long periods in solitary confinement. The following is an extract from a circular letter which Richard Steele sent to friends on 17 May 1981 shortly after his release from detention.

Dear Friends,
It is marvellous to be home, to be in a warm, accepting environment once again. Thank you for all your concern and faithful support for me and my family while I was in Detention Barracks. Hardly a day would go by without their being some card or letter for me in the post — all in all I received over 1400 pieces of mail during my twelve month stay. Besides the enrichment your letters and cards brought me, I am sure they were also a great witness for peace to those military authorities who read them first.

Some reflections on and learnings from my year behind bars and barbed wire:

· For all the heartache of being physically separated from the everyday love of my friends and family, the frustration of not being able to do 'normal' things like listen to music, eat yogurt, walk through town, chat with new people; the pain of being constantly surrounded by the harshness of the military machine . . . this was a growth year for me. I am greatly enriched through what I learned in that experience about myself, about God, about my relation to him, to my fellow beings and to creation as a whole.

· I was deeply touched by the sense of brotherhood I felt with my fellow prisoners, a solidarity in shared oppression which eclipsed personal differences. Through being open to one another, we kept burning the flame of love and caring even though prison ugliness sought to stamp it out.

· 'It is exciting to experience now the actuality of what before was largely theoretical for me — to make concrete and refine it. It is a joy actually to *be* obedient to Christ in his way of love and gentleness. It feels very good to *say* 'I love my neighbour' and to *do* it by refusing to participate in war or training for war. My vegetarianism, too, is a way in which I *live out* the principle of Reverence for Life which I so firmly believe in. Thus, even in the midst of the psychological, emotional and physical pressures and tensions I do experience in this situation, I am deeply at peace within myself and with those around me because of the congruence between my beliefs and actions in this instance, and the knowledge that by my non-cooperation with war structures, I am lowering the general violence in our world if only by an infinitesimal degree' (written in a letter home, November, 1980).

· I have learned that it is not enough to espouse a position or point of view merely verbally (even though it may, in fact, be a good one) and expect it to be listened to and accepted at face value. For it to be credible and influential the point of view must be personally embodied, given practical, lifestyle support. It is the day-to-day living out of our beliefs which carry weight and have moral authority.

If anything, my experience last year deepened my belief in and commitment to the path of Christian pacifism. Through my observation in the Detention Barracks' environment of the dehumanising effects on people of violence, and through my own experience of the psychological violence, amongst other things, of solitary confinement, my conclusion is that, for me, as a footstep-follower of Jesus Christ, violence in whatever form and in whatever way it may be used, is bad and wrong. It is wrong because it is antithetical to God's command to love all people with an unselfish, sacrificial love. Violence harms and destroys life so it is an insult to God who is the Giver of Life and whose image is reflected in every person who is made. Doing violence contradicts our calling as Christians and humans to be bearers of life and nullifies any claim by the church to be a reconciled and reconciling community. I now believe more firmly than ever that the Christlike way of forgiveness, love, gentleness and servanthood is right and glorifying God because it allows each person the freedom to grow into the fullness of life which God intends for us, and is the true way to meaningful, constructive human relationships and a genuinely meaningful and just society.

Yours in the solidarity of love.

Richard

Happy the peacemakers

Matthew 5:1-12 (JB)

Seeing the crowds Jesus went up the hill. There he sat down and was joined by his disciples. Then he began to speak. This is what he taught them:

'How happy are the poor in spirit;
theirs is the kingdom of heaven.
Happy the gentle:
they shall have the earth for their heritage.
Happy are those who mourn:
they shall be comforted.
Happy those who hunger and thirst for what is right:
they shall be satisfied.
Happy the merciful:
they shall have mercy shown on them.
Happy the pure in heart:
they shall see God.
Happy the peacemakers:
they shall be called the sons of God.
Happy those who are persecuted in the cause of right:
theirs is the kingdom of heaven.

Happy are you when people abuse you and persecute you and speak all kinds of calumny against you on my account. Rejoice and be glad, for your reward will be great in heaven; this is how they persecuted the prophets before you.

An instrument of peace

A Zulu interpretation of St Francis' Prayer
by P.T. Manci[69]

High voices

Nko - si, nge - nze isi - kha - li so - xo-lo.

Low voices

Nkosi ngenze isikhali soxolo.
Nkosi ngenze isikhali soxolo.
Nkosi ngenze isikhali soxolo.

1 Make me, O Lord, an instrument of peace,
  Where there is hatred, let me bring love,
  Where there is sorrow, let me bring joy,
  Where there is fighting, let me bring peace.   *Nkosi . . .*

2 Help me forget myself, help me to see
  Oppression and suffering, help me to know,
  Help me to understand, give me your eyes.   *Nkosi . . .*

3 Where there is anger, let me bring calm,
  Where there is hunger, let me be sharing,
  Where there is loneliness, let me bring care.   *Nkosi . . .*

4 Help me cross over every division,
  Barriers of wealth or race, language or creed,
  It's your will to break them down, let us be one.   *Nkosi . . .*

---

[69] Translated by Fr. Dave Dargie.

26

Redemptive Suffering

The Christian life is ultimately sharing in the suffering of Christ. Christians often find themselves caught in the cross-fire of opposing factions, seeking to bear witness to the reconciling power of the cross. But this witness, which literally means 'martyr', is one of costly identification with the redemptive suffering of Christ for the world.

The example of Christ   1 Peter 2:21-25 (NIV)

It is commendable if a man bears up under the pain of unjust suffering because he is conscious of God. But how is it to your credit if you receive a beating for doing wrong and endure it? But if you suffer for doing good and you endure it, this is commendable before God. To this you were called, because Christ suffered for you, leaving you an example, that you should follow in his steps.

> He committed no sin,
> and no deceit was found in his mouth

When they hurled their insults at him, he did not retaliate; when he suffered, he made no threats. Instead, he entrusted himself to him who judges justly. He himself bore our sins in his body on the tree, so that we might die to sin and live for righteousness; by his wounds you have been healed. For you were like sheep going astray, but now you have returned to the Shepherd and Overseer of your souls.

Power beyond words

Manas Buthelezi[70]

Not all suffering is redemptive. Most of the suffering in the world is oppressive. When people suffer as a result of the harm they do to themselves and to their neighbours such suffering is oppressive. According to the language of the Bible it is suffering which comes as a consequence of sin, since the wages of sin is death. 'For what credit is it, if when you do wrong and are beaten for it you take it patiently?' (1 Peter 2:20). It is oppressive suffering because it entangles the victim in the chain of his actions. What is true of the individual is also true of society. If a society is fundamentally unjust suffering will result, but such suffering will be part of the treadmill of perpetrating injustice, a vicious circle.

People also suffer as a consequence of the sin of others. Those who are on the receiving end of injustice and oppression suffer, but their suffering is oppressive and not necessarily redemptive. Suffering becomes oppressive when the victims accept it as a destiny. When the oppressed, knowing no better life, come to accept their lot as normal and even experience moments of happiness and satisfaction within it. When suffering attains the capacity of dimming the victim's perception of it, it becomes oppressive.

Oppressive suffering does not belong to the category of the suffering of Christ on the cross. Christ's suffering on the cross was redemptive. It was for the sake of others beyond the self. It was suffering which was occasioned by love and the circumstances of the other. 'Greater love has no man· than this, that a man lay down his life for his friends' (John 15:13). On the cross God transformed the experience of suffering at the hands of unprovoked violence into a medium of redemption. Through the cross God transformed the instrument of violence, vengeance and death into a vehicle of divine love and restoration to new life.

In the church we have become used to associating the gospel with certain words and even a certain formula of truth. We speak of the Word of God and the power of the

[70] From Manas Buthelezi, 'Violence and the Cross in South Africa Today', *Journal of Theology for Southern Africa*, no. 29, December 1979, pp.51f.

Redemptive suffering

Word of God. We attach a lot of importance to the verbalization of the saving reality to the point where we even forget that Christ's cross was a step beyond words. It was the extension of the speech of prophecy into the power of silent redemptive suffering.

When the ministry of words has lost its efficacy prophets may be called upon to communicate the saving message through the substance of their lives, that is, through the ministry of suffering. Beyond prophecy lies the cross. You can shut your ears to words, but you cannot escape the impact of a redemptive life. Redemptive suffering is power beyond words. This consists in putting your life at stake for the welfare of others.

If the cross is power beyond words the resurrection is the powerful hope that liberation lies beyond the experience of suffering. There is Easter beyond Good Friday. Easter is not always a dramatic feast that comes three days after Good Friday. There are many to whom the whole of life seems to be a long Good Friday. I am thinking of those who are suffering as I speak, not because they killed somebody or did something wrong, but because they dared to live a vicarious life of championing the interests of their fellows. Robert Sobukwe died before he saw the day of liberation for which he had sacrificed the security and normal life of adult years.

It is a misunderstanding to associate the suffering of Christ only with Good Friday. His whole life was a life of suffering and bearing other people's burdens. To care about other people's problems in addition to your own can be a heavy burden indeed. To care only about yourself and your problems can make life very simple. But once you allow other people's problems to worry you and to create an impact upon your life, then you end up suffering with them. That is redemptive suffering. When you allow even your own suffering to become a window through which you gain access to the suffering of others, that is vicarious living. This is the meaning of the cross. This is to take up one's cross and follow Christ.

We know love

Noorie Cassim[71]

Oh people you shall not drown in your tears
But tears shall bathe your wounds.

Oh people, you shall not die from hunger
But hunger shall feed your souls.

Oh people, you are not weak in your suffering
But strong and brave with knowing.

Oh people, if you have known struggle
Only then are you capable of loving.

Oh people, be aware of the love you have

Let not your tears submerge it
Let not your hunger eat it
Let not your suffering destroy it —

Oh people, bitterness does not replace a grain of love:
Let us be awake in our love.

We are healed by his suffering

He endured the suffering that should have been ours
   The pain that we should have borne.
Because of our sins he was wounded,
   Beaten because of the evil we did.
We are healed by the punishment he suffered,
   Made whole by the blows he received.
God commends his love to us in that, while we were yet
   sinners, Christ died for us
   Behold the Lamb of God, who takes away the sin of the world.

---

[71] Norrie Cassim, 'We Know Love', *The Return of the Aamasi Bird*, p.336-7. First published in *Staffrider*, March 1979.

Beyond Bitterness and Despair

The Christian life is not easy. Christians are not immune to the temptation to become embittered by those who attack or slander them in deed or word, nor untouched by the temptation to lose heart and hope in the struggle for what is right and true. But we are called to live beyond such bitterness and despair because these not only undermine our witness but also destroy our souls.

How long, O Lord

Psalm 13

How long, O Lord, will you so utterly forget me:
how long will you hide your face from me?

How long must I suffer anguish in my soul,
and be so grieved in my heart day and night:
how long shall my enemy triumph over me?

Look upon me, O Lord my God, and answer me:
lighten my eyes, lest I sleep in death;

Lest my enemy say 'I have prevailed against him':
lest my foes exult at my overthrow.

Yet I put my trust in your unfailing love:
O let my heart rejoice in your salvation.

And I will make my song to the Lord:
because he deals so bountifully with me.

We do not lose heart

2 Corinthians 3:17-4:18 (NIV)

Now the Lord is the Spirit, and where the Spirit of the Lord is, there is freedom. And we, who with unveiled faces all reflect the Lord's glory, are being transformed into his likeness with ever increasing glory, which comes from the Lord, who is Spirit.

Therefore, since through God's mercy we have this ministry, we do not lose heart. Rather, we have renounced secret and shameful ways; we do not use deception, nor do we distort the word of God. On the contrary, by setting forth the truth plainly we commend ourselves to every man's conscience in the sight of God. And even if our gospel is veiled, it is veiled to those who are perishing. The God of this age has blinded the minds of unbelievers, so that they cannot see the light of the gospel of the glory of Christ, who is the image of God. For we do not preach ourselves, but Jesus Christ as Lord, and, ourselves as your servants for Jesus' sake. For God, who said, 'Let light shine out of darkness,' made his light shine in our hearts to give us the light of the knowledge of the glory of God in the face of Jesus Christ.

But we have this treasure in jars of clay to show that this all-surpassing power is from God and not from us. We are hard pressed on every side, but not crushed; perplexed but not in despair; persecuted, but not abandoned; struck down, but not destroyed. We always carry around in our body the death of Jesus, so that the life of Jesus may also be revealed in our body. For we who are alive are always being given over to death for Jesus' sake, so that his life may be revealed in our mortal body. So then, death is at work in us, but life is at work in you.

My seven lean years

C.F. Beyers Naude[72]

On 19 October 1977, Dr. Beyers Naude was banned by the South African government along with the Christian Institute of which he was Director and other members of the staff. Banning meant that he was

---

[72] C.F. Beyers Naude, 'My Seven Lean Years', *Journal of Theology for Southern Africa*, no. 51, June 1985, pp.10ff.

isolated from social contact, restricted to the magisterial district of Johannesburg, unable to publish or to be quoted. The banning lasted seven years, until 16 September 1984. The following extract is from Dr. Naude's speech, 'My Seven Lean Years' which he gave at the University of Cape Town on the occasion of his seventieth birthday in May 1985.

There was also the practical side of a banning order. It has to do with facing one's feelings of anger, frustration, and vindictiveness which inevitably arise. I soon discovered that I had to make a crucial decision with regard to these feelings: would I allow these feelings to take root in my life, or would I do everything in my power to ensure that no such feelings would corrode my inner life and freedom? I requested my wife, Ilse, to be on the outlook for any signs of such expression of anger or bitterness and to help me to discover this immediately she became aware of such expressions. This she faithfully did, and for this I thank God, and as far as I know both of us have been able to live through this period and to conquer any feelings of bitterness, hatred or revenge which otherwise could have destroyed us. I consciously refused to allow the banning order to accomplish its intended goal.

· It would not rob me of the opportunity to think, reflect and plan the future.

· It would not prevent me from sharing and passing on my insights, analyses, discoveries of new values to other people — even if this could only be done one at a time. Such discovery of precious thoughts and new truths were like small seeds which I was sowing all the time, certain in my faith that the explosive power of truth would let it take root and grow in the heart and minds of many of those with whom I associated during this period.

· It would not stop me loving people and trying to understand them better, deepening my concern for their hopes, their joys and their suffering and therefore becoming more sensitive to such joys and suffering.

· It would not stop me from growing as a human being and as a Christian.

· It would not rob me of my inner freedom, my peace of mind, my joy of living and sharing.

All of this brought me to the firm conclusion: through God's grace I would never allow this banning to break my spirit, to distort my freedom of mind, or my concern for justice. It would never rob me of the deep conviction, inspired by my Christian faith and my sense of justice as I discovered time and again through the pronouncements of the Old and the New Testament that freedom will come to our land, that the system of apartheid will eventually crumble and disappear, and that our country and our people will be free.

A spirit seized me

Colin Bowes[73]

A fire burns within my heart
consuming hope, strength and trust
Deep in my mind is a spark
of torment, frustration and fear.
Who can lift the yoke
of toil and turmoil?
Who can lift the curse
imposed on me from birth
and heal the wound
which never bleeds?
Who can break the chains
that bind me
to sin, misery and crime?

Have I become a thing amongst things?
A beast among creatures
and a tool among weapons?
I waited,
perhaps too long
to hear the wind whisper
'brother, you are free'.
The freedom to listen to justice
or a baby cry
or a leaf falling from a tree.

[73] Published in *Pro Veritate*, July 1971, p.2.

And as I pondered
on these things,
the fire within me became a flame
causing eery shadows.
Shadows of hate, vengeance and pride.

I gazed at the mute gods
standing on their granite bases
their eyes as cold as death.
They just stood there
as they did centuries ago.

Suddenly a cloud covered them
and I saw them no more.

I rose up for action —
but the flame died out,
and the world laughed at me
from Sinai to Simonstown.

I cursed the day
the night and the hour,
I shunned humility.
And when I knelt
as if in prayer
my dark hands raised on high,
a spirit seized me
ten times ten
with force and ecstasy.

A litany of rejoicing

A Service of Celebration, Cape Town, 16 July 1972

Leader: For rebirth and resilience,
People: Blessed be God;
Leader: For the spiritually humble,
People: Glory to God, Hallelujah;
Leader: For all who are hungry and thirsty for justice,
People: Praise him and magnify him forever;
Leader: For all who are banned for speaking the truth,
People: Blessed be God;

Leader: For all who triumph over their bitter circumstances;
People: Glory to God, Hallelujah!
Leader: For all who risk reputation, livelihood and life
        itself for Christ's sake and the gospel;
People: All praise and all glory; this is God's kingdom;
        praise him and love him forever. AMEN.

28

Forgiving Love

The Christian life is lived on the basis of the forgiveness of our sins. The Christian always remains a sinner, yet one who has accepted the forgiveness of God. The Christian life is one of forgiving others just as we have been forgiven. Forgiveness means accepting another person in love despite what that person is or has done.

The unforgiving servant

Matthew 18:21-35 (NIV)

Then Peter came to Jesus and asked, 'Lord, how many times shall I forgive my brother when he sins against me? Up to seven times?' Jesus answered, 'I tell you, not seven times, but seventy-seven times. Therefore the kingdom of heaven is like a king who wanted to settle accounts with his servants. As he began the settlement, a man who owed him ten thousand talents was brought to him. Since he was not able to pay, the master ordered that he and his wife and his children and all that he had be sold to repay the debt. The servant fell on his knees before him. "Be patient with me," he begged, "and I will pay back everything." The servant's master took pity on him, cancelled the debt and let him go. But when the servant went out, he found one of his fellow servants who owed him a hundred denarii. He grabbed him and began to choke him. "Pay back what you owe me!" he demanded. His fellow servant fell to his knees and begged him, "Be patient with me, and I will pay you back." But he refused. Instead, he went off and had the man thrown into prison until he could pay the debt. When the other servants saw what had happened, they were greatly distressed and went and told their master everything that had happened. Then the master called the servant in. "You wicked servant," he said, "I cancelled all that debt of yours because you begged me to. Shouldn't you have had mercy on your fellow servant just as I had on you?" In anger his master turned him over to the jailers until he should pay back all he owed. This is how my heavenly Father will treat each of you unless you forgive your brother from your heart.'

A commission to forgive   David du Plessis[74]

David du Plessis, South African born Pentecostalist leader, has pioneered the entrance of the Pentecostal churches into the ecumenical movement. Known worldwide as 'Mr Pentecost', Pastor du Plessis has become loved and respected in many different churches and denominations, and was an invited observer at Vatican II.

Luther once exclaimed: 'Where forgiveness of sins is, there is life and blessedness.' The certainty of forgiveness in Christ is the secret of Christian life and joy. But it creates vast difficulties for the modern mind. Evangelism is the good news of forgiveness from sins. But how can you bring the evangel to people who are quite comfortable and have no conscience? God made provision for that. The Spirit is very active. Jesus said: 'When the Spirit is come, he will reprove the world of sin.' In fact he said : 'It is expedient for you that I go away. If I go not away, the Spirit will not come to you. But when I go away, he will come and he will reprove the world of sin.' What is so expedient about that? Then *you* don't have to reprove the world of sin. *You* can be the people that save the world from sin. 'I came not to condemn the world, but to save the world.'

There came a day when God challenged me to go to my brethren in other churches, 'But Lord, they are dead.' He

[74] An edited extract from David du Plessis, 'The Holy Spirit and Evangelism', in Michael Cassidy (ed.) *I will Heal their Land*, Africa Enterprise, Pietermaritzburg, 1974, pp.292f.

said: 'Yes, but I never sent any disciples to bury the dead. I sent them to raise the dead,' 'But they're enemies.' God said: 'I gave you an invincible weapon against your enemies. *Love* your enemies.' I said: 'How can I love people that do things I cannot approve of?' He said: 'Forgive them. Forgive them.' I said: 'Lord, I can't forgive them. How can I justify their teachings, their actions, their deeds?' He said: 'I never gave you any authority to justify anybody. I gave Christians authority to forgive everybody.' And then I began to check the Scriptures.

'Receive the Holy Spirit. If you forgive the sins of any, they are forgiven; if you retain the sins of any, they are retained.' I did not know for many years that *this* is the basis of Christianity. I had tried as hard as any to carry out the great commission, but *this* commission I had completely overlooked, and I had never heard a sermon on it either. In fact, the only story I heard once was that this was a special privilege for the apostles only. I declare that this is the Christian life of *everyone* who receives the Spirit. Anyone that becomes a child of God by regeneration through the Holy Spirit, from that moment on has been redeemed, has been forgiven his ten thousand talents, and now it behoves him to forgive his fellows their ten pence.

I had begun to see that something was missing in my life. I was not a forgiving Christian. Why should Christianity have become the most condemning, judgmental society you can find anywhere? Christians judge each other, condemn each other; they seek to do what they call mission work, but have nothing but judgment and condemnation for the people they go to. They try to reform them, tell them their culture is no good, tell them their customs are no good, try to change them. Are they evangelising or are they Westernising? Is that the gospel? The gospel is forgiveness. Forgive.

Have you ever tried to forgive seventy times seven? How do we live with this matter of forgiveness? It became a very serious matter with me. I had to battle to see that I forgave all the Protestants everything I ever had against them as a Pentecostal. But I didn't know the Lord was going to take me further. In Rome he said to me: 'Don't minister to Catholics if you cannot love them. As long as you condemn them you are not loving. You cannot love if you don't forgive, the more you forgive the easier it is to love. Love is the fruit of the Spirit, and an unforgiving spirit ruins your love, but a forgiving spirit increases the fruit of the Spirit.' And so I forgave. But I said: 'Lord what about history?' I learnt history in South Africa and whether it was slanted or not, doesn't matter. I had a knowledge of history that made the Catholic Church a horror, I knew all about it. And the Lord said: 'I never appointed you as a judge of history either. Forgive history. Forgive it all.'

My friends, my life, I confess, was completely revolutionised from the day I began to practise forgiveness. But I find there is no end to it, if we truly, honestly practise what Jesus taught. . . . When he breathed his Spirit into my life he said: 'Forgive, forgive. Forgive until seventy times seven. Never, never judge people.'

A perplexing disease called love Mbuyiseni Oswald Mtshali[75]

There is a perplexing disease called Love,
which smites and confuses.
Whilst the world watches,
the lovers remain as blind as a mole:
they take the world
and make it completely theirs,
where they enjoy jokes
and tell funny stories.

> Love vaults over high mountain tops;
> it kicks every obstacle on its path;
> its success brings solace;
> it reaps the fruits of a blissful life;
> it burns with unbearable flames.

Love can dive under waves,
without spluttering, without floundering.
Monsters can howl with horror.

[75] Mbuyiseni Oswald Mtshali, *Fireflames*, Shooter and Shuter, Pietermaritzburg, 1980, pp.6f.

Love never cares;
it pushes ahead
as doggedly as dripping honey.

> Even if a gate is closed
> and secured with chains,
> when Love has been established
> it breaks the chains with ease,
> for the lover to kiss his precious love.

Although a deep chasm can be filled with large boulders to
    bar the way,
when Love has ripened,
and hope within the love remains unwithered,
Love will smelt the rocks
and reopen the old path of affection.

> Love smothers a person
> and turns him into a blind man.
> Though he may have eyes to see,
> Love conceals an obvious mistake
> which he will deny with vehemence,
> while he picks other people's faults,
> their hunch backs and sprouting pimples.

When darkness engulfs us,
Love lights the way;
it flashes the beasts
lurking in dark nooks and crannies.
They relax their standing manes;
danger is removed.
Love reveals the love
to his beloved.

> A river may burst its banks
> and submerge its ford.
> Love in its stubbornness
> will challenge the water
> and wade across with safety
> by kicking off fear and doubt.

Love comes from God

1 John 4:7-11 (JB)

My dear people,
let us love one another
since love comes from God
and everyone who loves
is begotten of God and knows God.
Anyone who fails to love
can never have known God,
because God is love.
God's love for us was revealed
when God sent into the world his only Son
so that we could have life through him;
this is the love I mean:
not our love for God,
but God's love for us when he sent his Son
to be the sacrifice that takes away our sins.

Lord, teach us to love

John de Gruchy

It is easy, Lord, to mouth the word,
to say 'I love'
but not practise what it means.

When we see the true love of a lover,
the extent to which such love
is prepared to go for the beloved,
to vault over mountains
and dive under waves,
we know our love is paltry,
self-seeking,
a denial of the word.

When we consider your love,
the love of the cross,
the descent into the depths of hell
in search of us,
your forgiveness which overwhelms
and heals us,
we know our love is cheap,

our forgiveness empty,
judgmental and graceless.

Teach us to love you
with heart, soul and mind,
to love our neighbour
and our enemy.
Teach us to forgive
as you have forgiven us.

Love your neighbour

Xhosa Group composition, Langa, Cape Town, 1979

Thanda ummelwane — Thanda ummelwane wakho,
   njengokuba uzithanda.
Thanda uThixo wakho — Thanda uThixo wakho
   ngentliziyo yakho yonke.

(Love your neighbour as yourself — love your neighbour
   as yourself
Love your God with all your heart.)

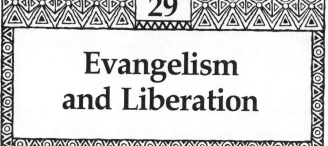

29

Evangelism and Liberation

The Christian life is to be shared with others in the power and love of the Spirit. Evangelism is proclaiming the good news of Jesus Christ in word and deed so that others may discover his grace and salvation. The proclamation of Jesus is especially good news to those who are poor or oppressed, but it is good news for all who acknowledge their need of God. Jesus came to liberate all of us from whatever bondage and blindness destroys our lives, and to give us life to the full.

Disciples of all nations
Matthew 28:16-20 (NIV)

The eleven disciples went to Galilee, to the mountain where Jesus had told them to go. When they saw him, they worshipped him; but some doubted. Then Jesus came to them and said, 'All authority in heaven and on earth has been given to me. Therefore go and make disciples of all nations, baptising them in the name of the Father, and of the Son and of the Holy Spirit, and teaching them to obey everything I have commanded you. And surely I will be with you always, to the very end of the age.'

The power of God
Acts 1:7-8, 2:32-33 (NIV)

Jesus said to them: 'It is not for you to know the times or dates the Father has set by his own authority. But you will receive power when the Holy Spirit comes on you; and you will be my witnesses in Jerusalem, and in all Judea and Samaria, and to the ends of the earth.'

Peter said: 'God has raised this Jesus to life, and we are all witnesses of the fact. Exalted to the right hand of God, he has received from the Father the promised Holy Spirit and has poured out what you now see and hear.

The Jesus way
Michael Cassidy[76]

Unfortunately some sincere Christians seem to act as if the Great Commission supersedes the Great Commandment. However, while New Testament love certainly obligates us to share with our neighbours the greatest good news in all the world, the story of salvation and forgiveness in Christ, it does not stop there. It goes into any area of activity or initiative which are demanded by plain, straightforward compassion. Yet so many of my evangelical and charismatic friends seemed to ignore this. Obviously something was terribly wrong somewhere. It seemed increasingly to me that those who were advising the stance that Christians keep their hands out of such unspiritual things as politics, economics and the problems of society, were often concerned not so much for the souls of men and the spirituality of religion as they were for their own freedom to do as they pleased in social, economic and political matters.

The structural question to me as a South African Christian was one which became a particular challenge. It seemed that South African structures were not only frustrating true social progress but also full human happiness and dignity. Should they not therefore be challenged? Especially when one saw a generation of young blacks slowly turning away from the Christian gospel because it seemed to have no relevance to the issues and pains they were facing.

---

[76] Michael Cassidy, *Bursting the Wineskins,* Hodder & Stoughton, London, 1983, p.205. Michael Cassidy is leader of African Enterprise, based in Pietermaritzburg, an evangelical organisation committed to evangelism throughout Africa but particularly in South Africa.

In the power of the Spirit
Bill Burnett[77]

This is an extract from the charge delivered by the Most Revd. Bill Burnett on his Enthronement as Anglican Archbishop of Cape Town in 1974. Bishop Burnett has been a leader in the Charismatic Renewal in South Africa.

Can we be foolish enough, faithful enough, to trust God and put ourselves, our present and future, into his hands? Unless we do that we cannot be said to believe in him. If we will, we can experience a new revelation of his love and a revolution in relationships in our land. He can deliver us all from our own past history, and this is a liberation we all sorely need.

I testify, as I am sure many of you can, that I have seen and heard in these last years what the dynamic of God can accomplish by his Holy Spirit. God is doing a new thing which is also a very old thing: we have always known about his power but we may experience the full and liberating blast of his love through the Holy Spirit.

Our failure is that of unbelief. Our failure is not so much that we are bad neighbours, bad legislators or prejudiced people, but that we do not believe in the power of God. It is palpably unfair to browbeat the man in the pew for his sub-Christian racial attitudes and for his refusal to share economic and political power, or for his failure to look another man in the eye because he is not conscious of his own worth, if we do not bring him to such a knowledge and experience of God as will set him free to respond to the love of God and the needs of his neighbours.

It is also irrelevant to talk about the witness of the church in society unless Christians are taught not only to know *about* but also so to *experience* God's love as to be led by it to pursue justice. It is moreover palpably unfair for Christians simply to blame Governments when the church is not demonstrating in its own life that quality of God's love from which justice may be born. If we are not being healed in the

[77] From Archbishop Bill Burnett's enthronement charge, published in *Seek*, September 1974.

church how can we exercise an effective ministry for the healing of society, and from where will come those who can be for the healing of the nation?

Liberation as a gift of grace Albert Nolan[78]

Evangelism is the transformation of the world in terms of an all-embracing vision of the divine kingdom. Gospel-liberation is not another form of liberation alongside all other more limited and partial forms of human liberation; it is all of these and more. If the kingdom is not *only* the salvation of souls and concerned not *only* with the next world, and if the kingdom represents the ideal of a complete, total and everlasting liberation, then it must include *every* partial form of liberation. That is why the Bishops Synod of 1971 could say: 'Action on behalf of justice and participation in the transformation of the world appear to us as a *constitutive dimension* of the preaching of the Gospel.'

This has far-reaching consequences for the church and its activities and for Christian behaviour in the world today. It means that evangelisation and the struggle for human liberation *coincide*. It means that evangelisation includes taking part in the various struggles for genuine liberation that are taking place in the world today. The only difference is that evangelisation lays claim to a certain *totality* and *completeness* which one cannot say of any particular struggle in any particular country for any particular kind of liberation.

The basis of this claim to totality is the liberation from sin. The liberation proclaimed by Jesus is total because it attacks the root cause of all oppression, all slavery and all suffering, namely sin. The various movements for liberation and justice that tackle *only* the consequences of sin: poverty, homelessness, ignorance, discriminatory laws, unjust structures, are on that account particular, incomplete and precarious. The salvation promised by Jesus overcomes sin *and* the consequences of sin. The great tragedy of recent times is that we

[78] From Albert Nolan OP, 'Evangelisation and Human Liberation', in *Grace and Truth*, vol. 5, no. 4, December 1984, pp.164f.

have preached a partial and incomplete gospel: only salvation of souls and only the liberation from sin. The rest, the consequences of sin in the world, was left to secular movements and political parties. We neglected the all-important and distinctive gospel message of totality and completeness — one of the very things that makes the gospel message divine.

What can we conclude from this about the difference between human liberation and evangelisation from the point of view of grace? Both seem to be totally a matter of human effort and totally a matter of grace. The difference would be that the same events looked at from the point of view of human liberation are seen as mere human achievements; whereas when they are looked at from the point of view of faith in God's transcendent kingdom they can be seen as both totally human and totally divine, as both human actions and gifts of God. Evangelisation adds this dimension of grace to our understanding of liberation.

There are, then, some very profound links between human liberation and evangelisation, but also some equally profound differences. Evangelisation envisages a *totality* of liberation and salvation in the Kingdom of God; it calls us continually to *transcendence,* challenging us to go beyond all our human limitations; and it enables us to see the dimension of *grace* or divine gift in all human achievements.

A time to live

Steve de Gruchy and Frank Mallows[79]

1. *Solo:* *We come to celebrate Good News*
   We come to celebrate your love
   Our hearts shall sing, and our voices tell
   of Jesus our Emmanuel
   One with us in our world of strife.

Solo *We celebrate your life on earth*
   the gift that you give
   The words and deeds that liberate
   a new life to live.

Refrain A time to live
   A time to walk in the light
   A time to give
   A time to dance in your sight
   A time to work, a time to play,
   to laugh and cry

[79] Composed for Rondebosch Congregational Church, Cape Town, 1984.

to sing and pray.
A time to receive the gift you give of new life
— it's a time to live.

2. *Solo*   *We are in the presence of your love*
       We are in the presence of your tears
  And from despair we draw aside
  to gaze upon the crucified
  Bring to him all our guilts and fears
  We gaze upon the sacrifice.

Solo   *The gift that you give*
  The freedom from a broken past
    A future to live.

3. *Solo*   *We come to celebrate your joy*
       We come to celebrate your peace
  And together, joined as one
  We celebrate your risen Son
  A foretaste of your heavenly feast.
  We celebrate the empty tomb.

Solo   *The gift that you give,*
  The victory over death itself
    A new hope to live!

Visions and Dreams

The Christian life is one of prophetic vision. Not all have the gift of prophecy, but all Christians have been given the Spirit who enables us to see reality in a new way, and to live in expectation of the fulfilment of the dreams of the coming kingdom of righteousness and peace.

Prophecy and vision

Proverbs 29:18

Where there is no vision
the people perish. *(AV)*

Where there is no vision
the people get out of hand. *(JB)*

Where there is no prophecy
the people cast off restraint. *(RSV)*

Habbakuk 2:1-4 (RSV)

I will take my stand to watch,
and station myself on the tower,
and look forth to see what he will say to me,
and I will answer concerning my complaint.

And the Lord answered me
  'Write the vision;

make it plain upon tablets,
  so he may run who reads it.
For still the vision awaits its time;
  it hastens to the end — it will not lie.
If it seem slow, wait for it;
  it will surely come, it will not delay.
Behold, he whose soul is not upright
  in him shall fail,
  but the righteous shall live by
  his faith.

Acts 2:1-4, 14-21 (NIV)

Your sons and daughters shall prophesy.

When the day of Pentecost came, they were all together in one place. Suddenly a sound like the blowing of a violent wind came from heaven and filled the whole house where they were sitting. They saw what appeared to be tongues of fire that separated and came to rest on each of them. All of them were filled with the Holy Spirit and began to speak in other tongues as the Spirit enabled them.

Then Peter stood up with the Eleven, raised his voice and addressed the crowd: Fellow-Jews and all of you who are in Jerusalem, let me explain this to you; listen carefully to what I say. These men are not drunk, as you suppose. It's only nine in the morning! No, this is what was spoken by the prophet Joel:

'In the last days, God says,
I will pour out my Spirit on all people.
Your sons and daughters shall prophesy,
your young men will see visions,
and your old men will dream dreams.
Even on my servants, both men and women,
I will pour out my Spirit in those days,
and they will prophesy.
I will show wonders in the heaven above
and signs on the earth below,
blood, and fire, and billows of smoke.
The sun will be turned to darkness
and the moon to blood,

before the coming of the great and glorious day of the Lord.
And everyone who calls
on the name of the Lord will be saved.'

Holding on to the vision

Allan Boesak[80]

The book of the prophet Habbakuk begins with the cry:
'How long, Lord?' His world was one of injustice, destruction and violence. Habbakuk's cry is one of deep anguish
and endless pain, a cry of dark and helpless despair. It is a cry
for love and compassion, a cry for justice. In this situation
what does the prophet do?

He does not despair. He does not resign himself to the
situation. He does not caution the people to accept things
'because that's the way it is'. He knows only too well that is
not the way it should be. The prophet, rather, turns to God
who awakens the desire for justice in the heart of the
oppressed, who hears a self-description in their cries: 'I will
take my stand to watch.' There is certainty here, a sure faith
that cannot be shaken, even by the destructive, violent
powers that rule the world. For the vision must come; it must
become the reality of the world.

The prophet's vision tells him that the 'world' that the
powerful have structured is a lie, a rejection and denial of the
world that God created. The vision insists that the powers of
evil that control and manipulate this 'world' are *not*
invincible. They can be challenged. The vision reveals that
liberation from oppression and the realisation of human ful-
fillment for the poor are not empty dreams. They can become
reality. The vision is rooted in history and in the God of history.

The prophet's vision is a vision of the God of the exodus
who could not remain unmoved by the pain and suffering of
the people. God took sides — *for* the oppressed people and
against the power and military might of the pharaoh. The

[80] From Allan Boesak, *Black and Reformed: Apartheid, Liberation and the Calvinist Tradition,* Orbis, New York, 1984, pp.64ff. Dr. Allan Boesak is a minister of the Dutch
Reformed Mission Church and President of the World Alliance of Reformed Churches.

prophet's vision is a vision rooted in the God who uprightly defends the poor, who saves the children of those in need, who liberates the oppressed but crushes the oppressor (Ps. 72). It is a vision rooted in the God who 'breaks the bow of the strong soldier, but gives strength to the weak . . . lifts the poor from the dust, and raises the needy from their misery' (1 Sam. 2:4, 8).

The vision of the prophet is a vision of liberation: to be saved from oppression, despair, and the humiliation of perpetual poverty; to be redeemed from the need to crawl and lie in order to stay alive; to be released from the fear of freedom and from the mad desire to be like the rich. The vision of the prophet rejects the false security of slavery and accepts with faith and joy the promise of a new life. The vision of the prophet accepts the truth of one's own humanity and, most of all, calls only the living God 'Lord'.

The vision of the prophet does not conform to the patterns of this world. It does not revolve around glory and world domination. Nor does it find inspiration in the accumulation of wealth and the power of destructiveness. It, rather, finds its meaning in the lives of the poor and the oppressed, the weak and the downtrodden. The vision of the prophet is realised in the signs of the kingdom of God: in the lame who walk, the lepers who are cleansed, the blind who see again, and the poor who hear the good news preached to them (Matt. 11) — in the wonderful things that happen to the lowly visited by God.

It is this vision that inspires priests and nuns as they join the people of El Salvador, Nicaragua, Guatemala, and Chile as well as many other places where the struggle against injustice, oppression, and inhumanity continues. It is this vision that inspires the young in South Africa to face dogs, tear gas, detentions without trial, and gunfire for the sake of liberation and human fulfilment. It is this vision that inspires the oppressed everywhere in an environment of poverty, fear, informers, torture, imprisonment, and death. The realisation of the vision may seem slow. The vision, however, is not deceptive. It will be realised. Its realisation cannot be delayed.

I'll never get used to nightmares

Christopher van Wyk[81]

Me, I cry easily if you're hurt
and I would've carried the crosses
of both the murderer
and the thief
if they'd've let me
and I'd've lived then.

I grasp helplessly at cigarettes
during riots
and burn my fingers hoping.

My nose has never sniffed teargas
but I weep all the same
and my heart hurts
aching from buckshot.

My dreams these days are policed
by a million eyes
that baton-charge my sleep
and frog-march me into a
shaken morning.

I can't get used to injustice.
I can't smile no matter what.

I'll never get used to nightmares
but I often dream of freedom.

One person's dream is another's nightmare

John de Gruchy

The dream of the mighty for more power, of the rich for more wealth, is the nightmare of the powerless and poor. But the dream of the oppressed and poor for liberation is the nightmare of the powerful and rich. It has always been so in a world which is unwilling to share resources and to discern them as gifts not possessions. The dream of the oppressed is utopian, it is a vision of a better world. But it is this vision

---

[81] Christopher van Wyk, 'Injustice', *The Return of the Aamasi Bird*, p.356f. First published in *Staffrider*, April 1980.

which enabled the first Christians to face persecution. 'Then I saw a new heaven and a new earth.' It is the same vision which has motivated the prophets through the centuries, the vision of the kingdom of God inaugurated in Jesus Christ but yet to come in its fullness. But this vision threatens those who possess everything except the ability to share with others. The powerful and privileged fear the dreams of the poor and the visions of the prophets because they derive from the coming kingdom of God, God's purpose for his world. They are dreams and visions which are just and right, and will come true.

A nation needs a common vision, a shared dream. A dream which is no one's nightmare because it promises hope and life in a new way for all. The message of Pentecost is that all people, young and old, Jew and Gentile, black and white, rich and poor, are brought within the scope of God's action through the Spirit. All people may be transformed and so transcend the barriers of race and class which divide nations and turn the dreams of some into the nightmares of others. This is the promise of the gospel in our land, a vision of righteousness and justice. Without such a shared vision the people will perish, and all our dreams will become a nightmare.

Let justice roll

Amos 5:24ff
Setting and tune by
Students' Union for Christian Action

Chorus: But let justice roll like a river,
Righteousness like a mighty stream;
And let justice roll like a river,
Righteousness like a stream.

Listen to the Lord!
I despise your pious festivals
I hate your sacred meetings,
Listen to the Lord!

Listen to the Lord
I will not accept your offerings
I disregard your sacrifice
Listen to the Lord!

Listen to the Lord!
I cannot endure your instruments
I will not hear your empty songs
Listen to the Lord!

31

The Lateness
of the Hour

The Christian life is lived in the awareness that every moment is critical. The call to discipleship is always immediate, it dare not be postponed. Living between the times, Christians witness to the coming judgment which is always the prelude to salvation. This witness does not mean running away from reality but living now in responsible love and obedience.

Woe to the complacent

Amos 6:1-7 (JB)

Woe to those ensconced so snugly in Zion
and to those who feel so safe on the mountain of Samaria,
those famous men of this first of nations
to whom the House of Israel goes as client.
Make a journey to Calneh and look,
go on from there to Hamath the great,
then go down to Gath in Philistia.
Are they any better off than these kingdoms?
Is their territory larger than yours?
You think to defer the day of misfortune,
but you hasten the reign of violence.
Lying on ivory beds
and sprawling on their divans,
they dine on lambs from the flock,
and stall-fattened veal;
they bawl to the sound of the harp,

they invent new instruments of music like David, they drink
   wine by the bowlful,
and use the finest oil for anointing themselves,
but about the ruin of Joseph they do not care at all.
That is why they will be the first to be exiled;
the sprawlers' revelry is over.

Judgment begins with the church

1 Peter 4:7-11, 16-17 (NIV)

The end of all things is near. Therefore be clear-minded and
self-controlled so that you can pray. Above all, love each
other deeply, because love covers a multitude of sins. Offer
hospitality to one another without grumbling. Each one
should use whatever gift he has received to serve others,
faithfully administering God's grace in its various forms. If
anyone speaks, he should do it as one speaking the very
words of God. If anyone serves, he should do it with the
strength God provides, so that in all things God may be
praised through Jesus Christ. To him be the glory and the
power for ever and ever. Amen.

If you suffer as a Christian, do not be ashamed, but praise
God that you bear that name. For it is time for judgment to
begin with the family of God; and if it begins with us, what
will the outcome be for those who do not obey the gospel of
God?

The bell has already tolled

B.B. Keet[82]

*In 1961 a volume of essays written by white Dutch Reformed Church
ministers was published under the title* Delayed Action. *The first
essay was by Professor B.B. Keet of the Theological Seminary in Stell-
enbosch who, a few years earlier, had written the first major critique
of apartheid by a Dutch Reformed theologian. Keet's essay in* Delayed Action *was titled 'The Bell has already Tolled'. It is significant to
reflect on the fact that this sense of the urgency of the hour has been
felt for many years in South Africa.*

---

[82] *Delayed Action!* N.G. Kerkboekhandel, Pretoria, 1961, pp.5, 10.

There comes a time in history, in the history of the church as well, when words must end and be transformed into deeds. And if the time be serious enough, the deed will be an extraordinary one, that is to say, it will be other than under normal circumstances. We are living, it seems to me, in such a time, and if nothing more came forward than a new declaration of principles which guide the church in its approach to the racial problem of our country, we may come to the realisation that, however prettily and however purely these principles may be put, in practice they would mean nothing because they can no longer be applied.

We do not know whether there is still time, but we must hurry — the bell has already tolled — or we will lose everything for which we have striven in this country. And then I am not thinking in the first instance about our material prosperity but about our spiritual values. . . . It will not harm white South Africa to act justly and to love truth. However, if we continue on the road already taken, it can only lead to a tremendous pitting of strengths which will be fatal for both white and black.

The moment of truth   The Kairos Document[83]

The time has come. The moment of truth has arrived. South Africa has been plunged into a crisis that is shaking the foundations and there is every indication that the crisis has only just begun and that it will deepen and become even more threatening in the months to come. It is the KAIROS or moment of truth not only for apartheid but also for the Church.

When they called I would not listen
Zechariah 7:8-14 (NIV)

The word of the Lord came to Zechariah: 'This is what the Lord Almighty says: "Administer true justice; show mercy and compassion to one another. Do not oppress the widow

[83] Published by the Kairos Theologians, Braamfontein, 1985.

The lateness of the hour

or the fatherless, the alien or the poor. In your hearts do not think evil of each other."

'But they refused to pay attention; stubbornly they turned their backs and stopped up their ears. They made their hearts as hard as flint and would not listen to the law or to the words that the Lord Almighty had sent by his Spirit through the earlier prophets. So the Lord Almighty was very angry.

'"When I called, they did not listen; so when they called, I would not listen," says the Lord Almighty. "I scattered them with a whirlwind among all the nations, where they were strangers. The land was left so desolate behind them that no one could come or go. This is how they made the pleasant land desolate."'

Stormy clouds on the horizon

Howard Eybers[84]

Take away my house white man
I'll still love you

Let me slave in your kitchen
while my little ones long for me
I'll still love you

Let me enter at your back door
I'll still love you

Take away our beaches
we'll still love you

Look down at me and say INFERIOR
I'll still love you

Go on being cruel to me
insignificant black thing
I'll still love you

But white man there are stormy
clouds on the horizon
the ground is shaking with thunder

---

[84] Howard Eybers, 'I'll still love you', *Pro Veritate*, 15 July 1973, p.14.

sleepy moles are coming to life
black hearts are beating faster
blood is racing in veins
. . . and
we may still love you.

God save us all
Felicia Komai and Alan Paton[85]

Alan Paton's famous novel Cry, the Beloved Country, *written in 1947, has captured the imagination of many throughout the world in communicating the deep pathos of the South African situation. The following extract is taken from the concluding pages of the book set in dramatic form by Felicia Komai.*

Black man: And now for all the people of Africa,
   The beloved country:
   Nkosi Sikelel' iAfrika . . .
White man: God save Africa . . .
   But *he* will not see *that* salvation.
   It lies afar off, because men are afraid of it.
   Because to tell the truth, they are afraid
   Of him, and his wife, and those like Msimangu.
Black man: But what is evil in their desires,
   In their hunger? That men should walk upright
   In the land where they were born,
   And be free to use the fruits of the earth,
   What is there evil in it?
White man: Yet men *are* afraid; with a fear that is deep,
   Deep in the heart, a fear so deep
   That they hide their kindness
   Behind fierce and frowning eyes. They are afraid
   Because they are so few. And such fear
   Cannot be cast out, but by love.
Black man: Yet there is a man, who has in him no hate
   for any man,
   But one great fear in his heart: that one day
   When they are turned to loving they will find

[85] Alan Paton, *Cry, the Beloved Country,* Jonathan Cape, London, 1948. Felicia Komai's verse-drama was published by Edinburgh House Press, London, 1954, pp.77f.

We are turning to hating . . .
White man: Oh, the grave and sombre words! . . .
   God save us from the deep depths of our sins.
   God save us from the fear that is afraid of justice.
   God save us from the fear that is afraid of men.
Black man: God save us all . . .

White man: Look to the east . . . Watch it, and pray . . .
   For when the sun comes up over the rim,
   It will be done, they say . . .

   The sun tips with light
   The mountains of Ingeli and East Griqualand.
   The great valley of the Umzimkulu
   Is still in darkness, but the light will come there.
   Ndotsheni is still in darkness,
   But the light will come there also . . .
   For it is the dawn that has come,
   As it has come for a thousand centuries,
   Never failing . . .
      But when *that* dawn will come,
   Of their emancipation — from the fear of bondage
   And the bondage of fear —
   Why, that is a secret.

In wrath remember mercy   Habakkuk 1:2-4, 3:2 (NIV)

How long, O Lord, must I call for help,
but you do not listen?
Or cry out to you, 'Violence!'
but you do not save?
Why do you make me look at injustice?
Why do you tolerate wrong?
Destruction and violence are before me;
there is strife, and conflict abounds.
Therefore the law is paralysed,
and justice never prevails.
The wicked hem in the righteousness,
so that justice is perverted.

Lord, I have heard of your fame;
I stand in awe of your deeds, O Lord.
Renew them in our day,
in our time make them known;
in wrath remember mercy.

32

The Feast of the Age to Come

The Christian life is a sharing in the joyous banquet of the kingdom of God. Every time the Christian community shares the common meal of bread and wine it celebrates the victory of Jesus on the cross, his risen presence, and the promise of his coming reign.

The common meal
Acts 2:42-47 (NIV)

They devoted themselves to the apostles' teaching and to the fellowship, to the breaking of bread and to prayer. Everyone was filled with awe, and many wonders and miraculous signs were done by the apostles. All the believers were together and had everything in common. Selling their possessions and goods, they gave to anyone as he had need. Every day they continued to meet together in the temple courts. They broke bread in their homes and ate together with glad and sincere hearts, praising God and enjoying the favour of all the people. And the Lord added to their number daily those who were being saved.

A LOVE-FEAST[86]

The celebration of the eucharist is at the heart of Christian worship. The eucharist, instituted by Jesus on the night of his arrest, was set within the context of the weekly meal shared by Jewish males. In the

---

[86] On the *Agape* see Gregory Dix, *The Shape of the Liturgy*, Dacre, Westminster, pp.82f; and David Tripp, 'Love-Feast' in *The Westminster Dictionary of Christian Spirituality*, p.252f.

early church this practice was continued, though gradually the eucharist was separated from the common meal which became known as the agape or love-feast. Tertullian said that Christians praised God through these meals, especially arranged for the poor. During the meal they spoke from the Holy Scriptures or as it was given them from the heart. In the church order of Hippolytus we read that the poor Christians were entertained by a wealthier Christian in his house and they 'broke bread'. This was called 'eulogia', blessing, instead of 'eucharistia', thanksgiving, because the eucharistic prayer of consecration was not offered. The agape has been used at various times during the subsequent history of the church. The agape has been particularly evident in times of persecution because it affirms Christian solidarity. It is also useful in ecumenical contexts where the eucharist is not possible. But it is not a substitute for the eucharist, rather it is the sharing of a meal, especially with the poor, within the context of worship, meditation and prayer. The following order for the agape has been adapted from that used by the Christian Institute in Cape Town. It should be altered to meet local needs, and hymns may be added where appropriate.

Preparation

Leader　We meet together
　　to confess our dependence on you, Lord;
　　our dependence on those great events in our history
　　which have shaped our attitudes and actions
　　both for good and evil;
　　our dependence on one another
　　in which we are powerfully influenced
　　to continue in good or evil;
　　and the dependence of others on us.
All　We meet together
　　in order that we might be created anew
　　as the people of God, the body of Christ.
　　We meet together
　　to commit ourselves
　　to share in Christ's redeeming work
　　in all the world.

Silent Reflection

The Word of God

Leader   Hear again of the great events
   and mighty voices
   whose impact has made our Christian heritage,
   and made us what we are.
   As we listen,
   we must also discern
   how to translate what we hear
   into significant action.
Let us pray:
All   Lord, your word has always come to us
   through events and insights in our human history.
   We commit ourselves now
   to listen and to speak
   so as to discover the truth
   that we may do it in love.

The Alpha and Omega   Revelation 21:1-6, 22:17, 20-21 (NIV)

Then I saw a new heaven and a new earth, for the first
heaven and the first earth had passed away, and there was
no longer any sea. I saw the Holy City, the new Jerusalem,
coming down out of heaven from God, prepared as a bride
beautifully dressed for her husband. And I heard a loud
voice from the throne saying, 'Now the dwelling of God is
with men, and he will live with them. They will be his
people, and God himself will be with them and be their God.
He will wipe every tear from their eyes. There will be no
more death or mourning or crying or pain, for the old order
has passed away. He who was seated on the throne said, 'I
am making everything new.' Then he said, 'Write this down,
for these words are trustworthy and true.' He said: 'It is
done. I am the Alpha and the Omega, the Beginning and the
End. To him who is thirsty I will give to drink without cost
from the spring of the water of life.

   The Spirit and the bride say, 'Come!' And let him who

hears say, 'Come.' Whoever is thirsty, let him come; who-ever wishes, let him take the free gift of the water of life. He who testifies to these things says, 'Yes, I am coming soon.' Amen. Come Lord Jesus.

A great banquet
Luke 14:12-24 (NIV)

Then Jesus said to his host, 'When you give a luncheon or dinner, do not invite your friends, your brothers or relatives, or your rich neighbours; if you do, they may invite you back and so you will be repaid. But when you give a banquet, invite the poor, the crippled, the lame, the blind, and you will be blessed. Although they cannot repay you, you will be repaid at the resurrection of the righteous.

When one of those at the table with him heard this, he said to Jesus, 'Blessed is the man who will feast in the kingdom of God.' Jesus replied: 'A certain man was preparing a great banquet and invited many guests. At the time of the banquet he sent his servant to tell those who had been invited, "Come, for everything is now ready." But they all began to make excuses. The first said, "I have just bought a field, and I must go and see it. Please excuse me." Another said, "I have just bought five yoke of oxen, and I'm on my way to try them out. Please excuse me." Still another said, "I just got married, so I can't come."

'The servant came back and reported this to his master. Then the owner of the house became angry and ordered his servant, "Go out quickly into the streets and alleys of the town to bring in the poor, the crippled, the blind and the lame." "Sir," the servant said, "what you ordered has been done, but there is still room." Then the master told his servant, "Go out to the roads and country lanes and make them come in, so that my house will be full. I tell you, not one of those men who were invited will get to taste of my banquet."'

All We are thankful for this Word of God to us and we long to be true to its truth and live by its light.

At heaven's door

Mbuyiseni Oswald Mtshali[87]

This, or some other contemporary reading, may be used.

Something
is not right
there upstairs,
maybe the wrong
is down here.

I have
been knocking
at the Door
since I learned
how to pray.

There
is only silence.
Where are the servants —
I mean the angels?

I don't see them
peering through curtains
to see who is calling.

When
the Master at last
says
'Come in,'

Will they
let me in
through the front
or at the back entrance?

*Opportunity is now given for quiet reflection, sharing, and possibly a
guided meditation, based on these or other readings.*

---

[87] Mbuyiseni Oswald Mtshali, *Sounds of a Cowhide Drum*, p.44.

Intercessions

An opportunity is given for sharing concerns that may be included in the intercessions. The intercessions can take different forms, but there should be scope for extempore prayer.

Intercession for the sick, the sorrowful, the distressed and the lonely

Leader   Jesus said: 'Come to me all you who labour and are heavy laden and I will give you rest' *(Matthew 11:28)*.

In the light of these words we remember the loving,
    caring ministry of Christ to all in trouble
his healing of the sick
his comfort of the sorrowful and the distressed
his abiding presence to the lonely.

All   We repent for our carelessness, our insensitivity,
    our judgmental attitudes, our lovelessness.

We pray especially for those who have been named,
remembering with joy the truth that neither death, nor
    life,
nor angels, nor principalities,
nor things that may happen today,
nor things that may happen tomorrow,
nor powers, nor height, nor depth,
nor anything else in all creation,
will be able to separate us
from the love of God in Christ Jesus our Lord
    (Romans 8:38-39).

(Pause)

We commit ourselves to be more sensitive
to the needs of others,
to care more deeply and to love more tenderly.

Intercession for the church

Leader   Jesus said: 'Your light must shine in the sight of
men, so that seeing your good work, they may give
praise to your Father in heaven' *(Matthew 5:16)*.

In the light of this we give thanks for the liberating
light of the gospel entrusted to the church.

But we are repentant for our dismal failures;
our involvement in war,
our unreadiness to change,
our lovelessness.

All   We commit ourselves to strive to be true to Jesus
Christ,
to share in the building up of the church,
to share in its witness to the world.

Leader   Jesus prayed, 'May they all be one, Father
as you are in me and I am in you,
may they be in us,
so that the world may believe' *(John 17:21)*.

In the light of this word we repent for the divisions in
the church,
divisions caused by tradition, culture, race and class,
and we confess our own part
in destroying the unity of the body.

In thankfulness to all who work and pray
for the unity and renewal of the church,
striving passionately and with creative vision
to make fast the unity which the Spirit gives.

All   We commit ourselves to strive with them
to express more fully the unity which we have in Christ
in our relationships and attitudes,
in our leadership and participation,
so that the world might believe.

Intercession for society and those in authority

Leader   Micah said, 'This is what Yahweh asks of you,
only this, to act justly,
to love tenderly,
and to walk humbly with your God' *(Micah 6:8)*.

In the light of this we are repentant
for the unequal treatment of people of different race
and class,
of bannings without trial,
imprisonment without trial,
and of all actions which dehumanise and degrade.

All   We are repentant for the enforced separation of
people black from white;
husband from wife
parents from children.

We pray for those who dare to claim that such injustice
is the will of God.

We confess that we too are guilty and in need of
forgiveness.

Leader   Guide those in authority so that they may rule
with justice and mercy,
remove unjust laws
confound the ruthless and those who
refuse to heed your word.

We give thanks for every sign of your presence in our
society,
for those who care for the underprivileged
for those who care for the aged, the
orphans and the handicapped,
for those who restrain evil and protect
against crime . . .

All   We commit ourselves to strive to oppose
injustice, prejudice, discrimination and inhumanity,
and to show in our dealings with others
the liberation of true justice, love and
human dignity.

The Meal

All We meet together to share this meal,
may it express our love for one another
our commitment to each other
and point us beyond ourselves
to the needs of the world.

Leader The peace of the Lord be with you all

All And also with you.

At this point the Peace is shared followed by a time of silent reflection.

All We believe in the love, mercy and righteousness of
the Lord
and ask for grace to begin anew
May Christ be present as we share this meal
so that we may share in his life
May Christ renew us and our community
so that we may be a sign of his kingdom in the world.

*The leader passes the loaf of bread to the person next to him or her,
who breaks off a piece of the loaf, giving it to the leader, and so forth
amongst all present. The same with the cup.*

Leader As Jesus taught us, we pray together
All Our Father in heaven,
hallowed be your name,
your kingdom come,
your will be done,
on earth as it is in heaven.
Give us today our daily bread,
forgive us our sins
as we forgive those who sin against us.
Let us not be led into temptation,
and deliver us from evil.
For the kingdom, the power, and the
glory are yours,
now and forever AMEN.

Commission[88]

Leader	As we go into the world, let us proclaim to all people
All	*Let us bear witness to the good news:*
Leader	God the Father creates us human and united
All	*Hallelujah, God is our protector.*
Leader	God the Son blesses our humanity
All	*Hallelujah, Jesus is our brother.*
Leader	God the Spirit creates us free and for freedom
All	*Hallelujah, our land shall be free.*
Leader	People of God, do not believe you are inferior,
All	*We shall not bow down to apartheid and its changing faces.*
Leader	People of God, work towards your future,
All	*We shall seek to be just rather than powerful.*
Leader	People of God, set up the pillars of justice, freedom and forgiveness in our land.
All	*We shall banish the false gods of race and tribe, class and sex from our midst.*
Leader	All people are created in the image of God and equal,
All	*Therefore apartheid is not God's will for us.*
Leader	Jesus Christ alone is Lord.
All	*Therefore the church of Christ defends the rights of the oppressed today and tomorrow.*
Leader	The Holy Spirit unites all the children of God
All	*Therefore we commit ourselves to living as one family of God in our land.*
Leader	We affirm: our warring, broken nation needs healing and wholeness:
All	*Black and white*
	men and women
	parents and children
	rich and poor
	soldier and soldier
	group and group,
	our fragmented country.

---

[88] From the Students' Union for Christian Action order for an *Agape*, based upon a Statement issued by the Alliance of Black Reformed Christians in South Africa.

God bless Africa,
guard her people,
guide her rulers,
and grant her peace.

Leader   'Now God's home is with all people! God shall live with them and they will be God's people. God will be their God, and will wipe away all tears from their eyes. There will be no more death, no more grief or crying or pain. The old has gone and the new has come.'   Amen.

All   *The grace of the Lord Jesus Christ, the love of God, and the fellowship of the Holy Spirit be with us all.*

ACKNOWLEDGEMENTS

Scripture texts
All scripture passages are identified by the following abbreviations:

JB *Jerusalem Bible,* © 1966, 1967 and 1968, Darton, Longman & Todd and Doubleday & Company Inc. Used by permission.

NEB *New English Bible,* © The Delegates of the Oxford University Press and The Syndics of the Cambridge University Press, 1961, 1970.

RSV *Revised Standard Version* © 1973 Division of Christian Education of the National Council of the Churches of Christ in the United States of America.

NIV *New International Version* of the Holy Bible copyright 1978 by International Bible Society. Used by permission.

Psalm extracts are taken from *The Psalms a new translation for worship (The Liturgical Psalter)* © 1976, 1977 English text David L. Frost, John A. Emerton, Andrew A. Macintosh, and published by Wm Collins.

Other texts
We are grateful to the following individuals and journals for permission to reprint their work: *Be Transformed, Between the Lines, Diakonia News,* Stephen de Gruchy, *Grace and Truth,* Janet Hodgson, *Journal of Theology for Southern Africa, Liberation (SACC National Conference Papers),* T.A. Mofokeng, Albert Nolan OP, Debora Patta, *Pro Veritate, Seek,* Gabriel Setiloane, *South African Outlook,* Leslie Stradling.

Hodder & Stoughton and Harold Shaw Publishers for *Bursting the Wineskins* by Michael Cassidy. Africa Enterprise for David du Plessis in *I will heal their land.* Baker Book House for *The Best of Andrew Murray* by Andrew Murray, © 1952 Fleming H. Revell. Wm. Collins Sons & Co., Fontana Paperbacks, Wm. B. Eerdmans Publishing Co.

and Skotaville Publishers for *Hope and Suffering* by Desmond Tutu. Wm. Collins Sons & Co., Fount Paperbacks for *Let My People Go* by Albert Luthuli. Shuter & Shooter (Pty) Ltd. for the poem *A perplexing disease called love* by Mbuyiseni Oswald Mtshali in *Fireflames*. A.D. Donker (Pty) Ltd. for *Sounds of a Cowhide Drum* by Mbuyiseni Oswald Mtshali. Orbis Books for *Black and Reformed: Apartheid, Liberation and the Calvinist Tradition* by Allan Boesak. Winston Seabury Press for *An Instrument of Thy Peace* by Alan Paton. C. Hurst & Co. for *Christians* by James Matthews in *Challenge of Black Theology in South Africa* published by John Knox. University Publishers for *Delayed Action* published by John Knox. SUCA News for *What I See in Egoli* (anon.). Wm. Heinemann for *Letters to Martha* by Denis Brutus. Ravan Press and Jeff Opland for *Xhosa Oral Poetry*. Ravan Press and Edgar Brookes for *A South African Pilgrimage*. Ravan Press and Hodge for *The Return of the Amaasi Bird* ed. Hodge.

Every effort has been made to trace the copyright owners of material included in this book. However, the author and publishers would be grateful if any omission in these acknowledgements could be brought to their attention, for correction in future editions.

INDEX OF BIBLE PASSAGES

All the passages, with the exception of those marked *, have been printed in full in the readings.

INDEX OF NAMES

INDEX OF READINGS, POEMS, PRAYERS AND HYMNS

259